The Seven Filters
Filtering your thoughts to align with God's will.

Steven B. Hankins, Th.D.

Copyright © 2023 Steven B. Hankins

All rights reserved.

ISBN – 9798850225728

Unless otherwise indicated, "Scripture quotations are from the ESV® Bible (The Holy Bible, English Standard Version®), copyright © 2001 by Crossway, a publishing ministry of Good News Publishers. Used by permission. All rights reserved."

Scripture quotations marked KJV, are from The Holy Bible, King James Version, 1611

Dedication

I dedicate this book to Seacoast Community Church and Columbia Missionary Baptist Church. These congregations provided cordial and valuable feed back as I covered this topic in brief during my time of ministry there.

I also want to recognize the first church that I joined after coming to faith in Jesus. While at the Alliance Church of Bartlett, I first pondered many of the thoughts in this book.

Contents

Preface 1

Introduction 3

Section 1 – Preparing to Hear from God 6

    Chapter 1 – The Capability to Hear 7

    Chapter 2 – The Mind of Christ. 15

    Chapter 3 – Hearing the Voice of the Lord 27

Section 2 – The Seven Filters 45

    Filter #1 – Am I living like a spiritual person? ... 46

    Filter #2 – Does the Bible say it is ok? 62

    Filter #3 – Are my methods correct? 78

    Filter #4 – Does it take true faith? 91

    Filter # 5 – What do other spiritual people think? ... 106

    Filter # 6 – Is my motive to glorify God alone? ... 122

    Filter #7 – Am I absolutely certain? 144

Conclusion 156

Works Cited 160

Preface

In 1983, while sitting in a Minneapolis Minnesota hotel room, the Lord saved me while reading a Bible placed by the Gideons International. It was the most glorious moment of my life. It was life changing.

I spent 33 years of my life being self-sufficient, running my own show. As I began assessing my life, I realized that in leading my own life I did a lot of damage to myself and, even more sadly, to others. Yes, many people were hurt in my path of destruction. It was not that I intended this but it was a natural result of running my own life.

As I sat on that bed in the hotel room reading the Bible, the Lord revealed all this to me. Oh, I knew the gospel, that Christ died to pay the penalty of my sin and that He rose again. However, up until that moment I did not realize how much I desperately needed a Savior. I could not save myself and I could not effectively lead my own life. So, I prayed a simple prayer.

The prayer went something like this. "Lord, I have sinned and need your forgiveness. Forgive my sin and save me. I want you in my life." I know that it was not much of a prayer. You see the prayer did not save me. It was the Lord who did this. The prayer was the outpouring of my heart. Yet I was not done. I continued, "I have been running my own life and have hurt a lot of people. I want you Jesus to be Lord of my life. Make my life a blessing. I need you to lead me in life. Amen."

My heart's desire was to stop leading my own life my way and to have Jesus lead my life His way. Yet this posed a problem. How? How would Jesus lead me. Let's face it, I made hundreds of decisions every day. How was I to know what Jesus wanted me to do?

Well, I became active in our local church. I went faithfully every week with my wife and children. I began learning things that I never previously considered. It was exciting. It was awesome.

However, then I heard some things in our circle of Christian friends. Things like, "God told me to do this." There was a young man, my age at that time, who I overheard in conversation. He had been a Vietnam conflict veteran. He was telling another believer in the church that God told him something and he immediately stopped what he was doing and wrote it down. I thought that was cool but frankly this confused me. Yet I was too embarrassed or proud to ask how he heard from God. Was it an audible voice? Was it a silent voice that only he could hear?

Down the road I began to understand this a bit better. There was perhaps an inner voice where the Lord in some mysterious way communicated with believers. The only problem I had was this. How do you know for certain that this inner voice is from the Lord? Could it be from our adversary the devil and not the Lord? Could it be from our own fleshly desires and not the Lord? To me this posed a very serious fear.

I discovered that we needed discernment. We make hundreds of decisions a day and have even more thoughts. These thoughts can lead us on the right path or they can also lead us on the wrong path. We need to be able to discern these thoughts and intents to ensure that the decisions we make and the actions we take are in line with the will of the Lord. So, I searched the Scriptures and discovered a few things that have significantly helped me to hear from the Lord and discern what I have heard.

I have written this book to help believers, both new and old, in two ways. The first is to help them understand how the Lord communicates with them. The second is to help them know how to filter their thoughts and ideas to ensure that are in alignment with the will of God.

Introduction

"We destroy arguments and every lofty opinion raised against the knowledge of God, and take every thought captive to obey Christ,"
(2 Corinthians 10:5, ESV)

In 1974, I graduated from Drexel University with a Bachelor of Science in Mechanical Engineering. After serving in the United States Army, I began working for a company in the printing and paper converting business. One of my assignments was as an assistant manager in the web printing department of a folding carton manufacturing facility in Illinois. As an engineer my primary responsibility was to oversee the technical aspects of the department and improve the production processes. Often the job involved investigating maintenance and production process issues on the machinery.

One day, one of our printing presses with an inline platen die-cutter started acting up. It would run for a few minutes and then shutdown. The oil pressure warning light on the die-cutter was the only thing that indicated a possible problem. Yet when we checked the oil level, we found everything was fine. After repetitive startups and shutdowns, we decided to check the oil filter. We thought it might be clogged but it looked fine. Then we thought that something must be clogged in the pipes that fed the oil to the cutter bearings. Checking this was going to be a major undertaking.

As we traced the oil system, we found a strainer in the oil pipe. The strainer was there to catch any large chunks of debris that might enter the system before they got to the filter. The strainer was in fact a coarse filter for this purpose. When we took the strainer out for inspection, we discovered the problem. Someone put a rag in the oil sump and when the machine started the rag was sucked up into the strainer. There it plugged up the oil circulating system, which triggered the low oil pressure warning switch and shut down the machine. The strainer did its job and kept the rag from getting sucked down towards the secondary oil filter.

In machine design it is common practice to place several filters in line like this. The first filter is usually cleanable, a porous mesh of some sort, designed to remove larger items, like nuts, bolts, metal shavings, and etcetera from getting to the next and finer filter. In this machine we had two filters to ensure the oil would be kept clean and prevent wear on the die-cutter bearings. Some processes have even more filters. Each one progressively removes finer and finer particles to ensure what comes out of the filters at the end is of the purest quality. This is what "The Seven Filters" is about.

We all have a multitude of thoughts every day. It is upon these thoughts that we act. Yet herein lies the problem. As believers in Jesus Christ how do we know if these thoughts are from the Lord, from our own fleshly desires, or from ungodly sources? There must be a way to know. If we could apply the appropriate filters to our thoughts then we would trap the ones that are not from God and eliminate them. In doing so we could ensure that only godly thoughts would get through the filters and guide our lives.

Paul wrote that we are to *"take every thought captive to obey Christ."* What follows in this book are two sections. The first section deals with the possibility of God speaking to believers and how to listen. The second section presents seven major filters for sorting out the believer's thoughts. Some of these filters will seem obvious. However, they are often forgotten in the busyness of life.

Christians of all levels of spiritual maturity must understand the vital nature of filtering out our thoughts. A failure to filter out our ungodly thoughts can bring on all kinds of evil, pain, and suffering. The Scriptures are full of examples of people who had not filtered their thoughts and acted on impulse. We have a sad

The Seven Filters

example of this seen in David's life where he committed adultery with Bathsheba. The Scriptures are also full of good examples of men who filtered out the thoughts imposed by the world system, their own desires, and evil forces. We see this in the true prophets of God who communicated the word of God regardless of the pressures placed upon them to compromise the truth.

"The Seven Filters" is a vital study for every believer. For the new believer it will prepare a foundation for seeking to know and do the will of God. For the mature it will hone their skills of discernment. It will make the Christian walk a more productive and joyous experience for all.

Steven B. Hankins, Th.D.

Section 1 – Preparing to Hear from God

Some of the greatest questions that believers have are these. Does God speak to us today? If He does, then how does He do it? Is it in an audible voice? Is it through circumstances? Can I really hear from God? I am certain that there are many other questions as well.

Let me say this. God does want to communicate with us today. The biggest questions are not regarding if He does communicate with us but how He does this.

More importantly, in addition to understanding how God communicates with us, we must understand our role in hearing from Him. Section 1, "Preparing to Hear from God," covers these vital considerations.

Chapter 1 – The Capacity to Hear ………………….. 7

Chapter 2 – The Mind of Christ …………………... 15

Chapter 3 – Hearing the voice of the Lord……………. 27

Chapter 1 – The Capability to Hear

"My sheep hear my voice, and I know them, and they follow me. I give them eternal life, and they will never perish, and no one will snatch them out of my hand." (John 10:27–28, ESV)

While in the Army I was stationed in Germany. For a while my wife and I lived in an apartment on what we called "the economy." This phrase referred to apartments rented by German people to soldiers, rather than property managed and provided by the United States government. The rental unit that my wife and I had was on the outskirts of a small country village right next to a large field.

On occasion a shepherd would bring his flock of sheep right down the street in front of our apartment to graze in the field. It was interesting to watch this shepherd work with his sheep. It was clear that he watched over them and they seemed to be attentive to his leadership.

Some years later I saw a sheep herding demonstration. The shepherd had a group of people standing by a fenced in area that contained his flock. The flock was some distance from the shepherd and the group. He then asked for a volunteer to call the sheep to come to where the group was standing. The volunteer called using the correct words but not even one sheep budged. Then the shepherd called for the sheep to come using the exact same words and the entire flock moved with purpose right up to the fence where he was standing.

This was one of the most dynamic demonstrations of what Jesus stated to a group of unbelieving Jews when He said, *"My sheep hear my voice, and I know them, and they follow me."*

Steven B. Hankins, Th.D.

Every true believer has had an experience of hearing Jesus' voice.

A lot of believers say that they have never heard the Lord speaking to them. However, according to Jesus' words this is not the case. The Lord stated, "*My sheep hear my voice, and I know them, and they follow me.*" Every true believer has had at least one dynamic experience of hearing the Lord's voice. It was the call to salvation. This calling to salvation is a theme repeated in the Scriptures. Jesus' "Parable of the Wedding Feast" pointed to this truth. He stated, "*For many are called, but few are chosen*" (Matthew 22:14, ESV). The chosen are those who have heard and responded to Jesus' call by faith.

We see this truth further reinforced in Jesus' words to the church in Laodicea.

> "*Behold, I stand at the door and knock. If anyone hears my voice and opens the door, I will come in to him and eat with him, and he with me*" (Revelation 3:20, ESV).

Those who receive eternal life are those who have heard Jesus' voice and opened the door to receive Him by faith.

The evidence of believers hearing the call of our Lord and responding by saving faith is that they become followers of Jesus. This implies a transition in life's priorities. After foretelling of His death and resurrection, Jesus presented this truth to the disciples.

> "*If anyone would come after me, let him deny himself and take up his cross and follow me. For whoever would save his life will lose it, but whoever loses his life for my sake will find it.*" (Matthew 16:24–25, ESV)

Yes, this is a tough saying but it shows the radical nature of faith in Jesus by those who have heard His calling. The disciples demonstrated such faith in a very literal way when the Lord called them. To Jesus' call, "*Follow me, and I will make you fishers of men,*" we see that "*Immediately they left their nets and followed him*" (Matthew

4:19–20, ESV). Their immediate response of dropping their nets and following Jesus is an example of the radical change that occurs in the hearts of those that hearken to the voice of our Lord.

So, what was it that all true believers have heard? Quite simply, it was the word of God concerning the gospel. If you are a believer who is following Jesus today, rest assured, you have had at least one occasion where you heard the Lord speaking to you. The evidence of this is that you have trusted in Him for eternal life.

Hearing from the Lord combines human faculties and divine provision.

One of our great questions is this. What is the mechanism by which one hears from the Lord? There is not just one factor in this. For the sake of understanding let us consider two broad and inseparable categories, the natural and the supernatural.

Now that I am a senior citizen, I have begun receiving a lot of junk mail targeted at my age group. I cannot count the number of mailings I have received regarding hearing aids. They will give a free hearing exam that will prove that I have a hearing problem. Frankly I do not need a free hearing exam since my wife tells me all the time that I must be deaf since I do not listen to her. Yet it is true, my hearing is not as good as it was 50-years ago. My eyesight is also not as good. Devices like glasses and hearing aids provide us with an ability to take in written and auditory information even when our eyesight and hearing diminishes. God has given us the Bible and the Holy Spirit so we can hear from Him. We just need to make our eyes and our ears attentive to the right things.

God has granted to man the revelation necessary to hear from Him. – From the natural side let us consider those things with which God has endowed every person. God has given to man what theologians call "general revelation." It is that revelation seen in nature through the creation itself. Paul described this in his letter to the believers in Rome.

"For what can be known about God is plain to them, because God has shown it to them. For his invisible attributes, namely, his eternal power and divine nature, have been clearly perceived, ever since the creation of the world, in the things that have been made. So they are without excuse." (Romans 1:19–20, ESV)

Moreover, God has given to man what theologians call "special revelation." Special revelation is the written word of God, the Bible. It is the truth of God that contains everything He wants us to know for life. The Psalmist wrote, *"The sum of your word is truth, and every one of your righteous rules endures forever"* (Psalm 119:160, ESV). Jesus echoed this thought in His high priestly prayer for the disciples, *"Sanctify them in the truth; your word is truth"* (John 17:17, ESV).

God has given man both "general revelation" and "special revelation" so people can know the truth. Because of this Paul wrote that man is without excuse (Rom 1:20), for everyone has some capacity to understand it.

God has endowed man with the faculties necessary to hear from Him. – In addition to general and special revelation, God has given man the intellectual capacity to comprehend, consider, and choose options. People have the capacity to receive and understand information through both written and spoken language. As far as receiving a word from the Lord we have the number one bestselling book of all time, the Bible. The Bible is the word of God. The word of God contains everything we need to know from God (2 Tim 3:16-17). Moreover, man has the God given intellectual ability to intake the Bible's truth, process it, and make choices based upon it.

Then what is the problem in hearing from God? It is not that God failed to equip man to intellectually grasp it. People of all intellectual levels can grasp the essentials. The primary problem is in the heart of a person. Sin has corrupted man's heart in such a way as to block the intellectual capacity to receive the truth. Referring to the Old Testament (Ps 14:1-3; 53:1-3) Paul stated, *"as*

The Seven Filters

it is written: "None is righteous, no, not one; no one understands; no one seeks for God" (Romans 3:10–11, ESV). God provides the revelation that man needs but man's heart is hardened against the truth of God. Thus, there are two possible problems. The first is that people may not spend sufficient time in the Bible. The second is that people may not be not in the spiritual condition necessary to comprehend the things revealed in the Bible.

God provides the supernatural manifestation necessary to hear from Him. – The Holy Spirit of God is the person of the Trinity who opens the heart to understand the truth of God. The major problem with man is not hearing the word of God proclaimed or reading the written word of God. It is one born in the heart that has been corrupted by sin. This spiritual blockage is what keeps the most intelligent people (from a human perspective) from comprehending the truth of the gospel. Those who do not believe when hearing the word or reading the Bible have a heart's predisposition against the truth of God.

The work of the Holy Spirit is fundamental in breaking through men's hardened hearts so they may be able to comprehend the truth of the gospel. Jesus had much to say concerning the Holy Spirit in this matter. In preparing the disciples for His departure, He called the Holy Spirit the *"Spirit of Truth"* (John 15:26). He further referred to this work of the Holy Spirit in opening the hearts of people to grasp the truth.

"And when he [the Holy Spirit] *comes, he will convict the world concerning sin and righteousness and judgment: concerning sin, because they do not believe in me; concerning righteousness, because I go to the Father, and you will see me no longer; concerning judgment, because the ruler of this world is judged."* (John 16:8–11, ESV)

The Holy Spirit would open the hearts of people to understand their sin problem, the righteousness of Jesus Christ who is the way, the truth, and the life (John 14:6), and the coming judgment for sin.

Furthermore, Jesus went on to tell the disciples that the Holy Spirit would be instrumental in their further understanding of God's truth.

> *"I still have many things to say to you, but you cannot bear them now. When the Spirit of truth comes, he will guide you into all the truth, for he will not speak on his own authority, but whatever he hears he will speak, and he will declare to you the things that are to come."* (John 16:12–13, ESV)

Jesus spoke of a time when the Holy Spirit would come upon them. This happened on the Day of Pentecost (Acts 2) and from that time on all believers were indwelt with the Holy Spirit at salvation (Rom 8:9-11). The Holy Spirit works to reveal the deep truths of God's word to all true believers. Theologians call this work of the Holy Spirit in giving believers the understanding of God's truth the doctrine of "illumination." It is that the Holy Spirit opens the hearts of believers to understand the truth of God as revealed in His word, the Bible. Here we are not speaking about new revelation but opening the hearts of people to comprehend the truths already revealed in the Bible.

While I served in the army, we would often be under blackout conditions. That meant no lights. I remember on one patrol being assigned as the point man for the platoon. While walking through the swamps, under the canopy of the trees, the only thing I could see was the luminescent markings on my compass dial. As I walked, I kept bumping into trees. Some were saplings. For the most part I could walk over or through the saplings. However, I ran into one that did not want to move. In fact, it sprung over and then lifted me up flipping me onto my back. Fortunately, my rucksack broke my fall. This would never have happened if I could have used a flashlight to illuminate my way.

Similarly, like a flashlight illuminates our way in the night, the work of the Holy Spirit illuminates the truth of the Scriptures in our hearts. This illumination of the Scriptures lights the way of righteousness so that believers can avoid straying from the safe path and wandering into the path of darkness and destruction. The Psalmist wrote that God's word *"is a lamp to my feet and a light to my path"* (Psalm 119:105, ESV). Paul indicated that it was the Spirit of God who illuminated the truth of the Scriptures for us.

> *"For who knows a person's thoughts except the spirit of that person, which is in him? So also no one comprehends the thoughts of God except the Spirit of God. Now we have received not the spirit of the world, but the Spirit who is from God, that we might understand the things freely given us by God."* (1 Corinthians 2:11–12, ESV)

Every believer has experienced this blessing of the illuminating work of the Holy Spirit. Otherwise, the believer would not have understood the gospel, its necessity, and responded to the message by faith.

Therefore, all true believers have heard the voice of the Lord calling them to saving faith. The voice of the Lord may have come from someone preaching the gospel message, or by reading the Bible, like I did, or by a variety of other means. Yet it was the ministry of the Spirit that illuminated this truth to the unsaved person's heart, which prompted understanding and saving faith.

When saved, every new believer experienced the indwelling manifestation of the Holy Spirit. Jesus stated that with this the believer is equipped to further receive and understand spiritual truth.

> *"But the Helper, the Holy Spirit, whom the Father will send in my name, he will teach you all things and bring to your remembrance all that I have said to you"* (John 14:26, ESV).

This is exactly how it works. When we study the Scriptures, when we read them, when we hear the word of God preached, seeds of truth are planted and the Holy Spirit illuminates them to us. Then when we need these truths in life the Holy Spirit brings them to mind. In this way God speaks to us so that we can make correct choices.

Therefore, the issue is one of believers growing in their knowledge of Scripture so they may be able to discern the thoughts and intents of their hearts.

Chapter 2 – The Mind of Christ.

"For who has understood the mind of the Lord so as to instruct him?" But we have the mind of Christ." (1 Corinthians 2:16, ESV)

In 1974, while pursuing a degree in Mechanical Engineering, I had to pass a required course in Nuclear Physics. It was highly theoretical. One of the things we had to do was memorize the derivation of Einstein's theory of relativity. The professor in the lecture hall proceeded to use four blackboards that stretched from one wall to the other in rushing through the derivation of this theory in one hour. He even ran out of space and was erasing with one hand while writing with the other. Even if we could memorize this derivation, we still needed to understand it. I was over my head. Unfortunately, I failed the course and had to retake it to squeak by with a passing grade.

Now imagine that I had the mind of Albert Einstein. I would not have failed the course the first time but would have aced it. In fact, I would have known the course materials better than the instructor. The point is this. Similarly, if we were to have the mind of Christ, we would be able to perfectly discern the voice of the Lord from all the other distracting voices that come in our thoughts. Our ability to know and follow the voice of the Lord would be a natural thing.

Yet here is the problem. While believers have the mind of Christ, we are still constantly growing in the same. Thus, as we grow in Christ our minds are increasingly developed so that we will respond in accordance with the will of God. So, the question is this. How does the believer grow in this ability?

Transitioning from Natural to Spiritual

When we look at the context of 1 Corinthians 2:16, we see that Paul makes a contrast between the natural person and the spiritual person. The natural person is the person without the Spirit, the unsaved person. On the contrary, the spiritual person has heard and responded to the calling of the Lord by saving faith. Simultaneous with saving faith every spiritual person experiences the indwelling manifestation of the Holy Spirit. Paul affirmed this truth in his writing to the Romans.

> *"You, however, are not in the flesh but in the Spirit, if in fact the Spirit of God dwells in you. Anyone who does not have the Spirit of Christ does not belong to him."* (Romans 8:9, ESV)

The Holy Spirit is the one who enables the saved person to hear and respond to the voice of the Lord. Paul indicated this in his letter to the church at Corinth.

> *"For who knows a person's thoughts except the spirit of that person, which is in him? So also no one comprehends the thoughts of God except the Spirit of God."* (1 Corinthians 2:11, ESV)

> *"The natural person does not accept the things of the Spirit of God, for they are folly to him, and he is not able to understand them because they are spiritually discerned. The spiritual person judges all things, but is himself to be judged by no one."* (1 Corinthians 2:14–15, ESV)

Thus, only true believers have the Holy Spirit and with this the mind of Christ by which they may understand the truth of God.

Yet while the spiritual person has a capacity to understand the truth that God has given, there is still a progression that occurs in the life of a believer. Paul further addressed this in the Corinthian letter.

> *"But I, brothers, could not address you as spiritual people, but as people of the flesh, as infants in Christ. I fed you with milk, not solid food, for*

The Seven Filters

you were not ready for it. And even now you are not yet ready, for you are still of the flesh." (1 Corinthians 3:1–3, ESV)

The believers in Corinth had not progressed in the faith. They were acting as infants in the faith and thus were not able to advance to the deeper truths from God. Paul wrote that there was one huge reason for this. They were driven by the flesh and not the Spirit. They needed to mature from this fleshly state to one of being driven by the Spirit. His description of them as infants in Christ illustrates the problem that new believers and those who have not progressed in the faith have.

I am now a grandfather and have five grandchildren. My most recent grandchild is a boy who, at the time of this writing, is just over two years old. As I have observed my own children and later my grandchildren, I have identified some basic characteristics of infants. The key one is that they are alive and are growing. Similarly, new believers are spiritually alive and should be growing in the faith. However, some new believers can become stunted in their spiritual growth. I have seen too many of these in my church experience. You look at them and expect much more maturity as demonstrated in their actions, especially when they tell you how long they have been saved.

Let us consider the characteristics of infants a bit more. They cry when they want something. They will do so without any recognition of the needs of others. There is no sacrifice of their own wants and desires for the sake of others. We frankly do not expect this from infants anyway. After all they are cute little helpless creatures who we expect to grow. In this process of growth parents nurture them and clean up their messes. Yet at some point children begin feeding themselves and eventually become mature adults. Believers who have not matured from infanthood, and there are many like this, are self-centered and have failed to grow in the knowledge and application of spiritual truth in life.

The ability to understand and apply spiritual truth to life is what having the mind of Christ is. Just as a newborn baby grows in the capacity to understand things and make decisions, newborn believers should be growing in their ability to understand the things of God and apply them to life. This is because every believer can grow in the faith. What is missing? It is generally the zeal to grow in the grace and knowledge of Christ. This is a critical work for every believer in developing the mind of Christ.

Developing the Mind of Christ

How does one mature and develop this ability to understand and apply spiritual truth? There are two basic elements to this. One has to do with the heart's focus and the other has to do with the believer's spiritual diet.

Believers must have a correct heart's focus. – To develop the mind of Christ believers must have a focus to walk in the victory Christ has already provided. This is the first essential. From one perspective this battle has already been won for us through the work of Christ on the cross. He has accomplished everything needed for us to live a life of godliness in this fallen world. He has defeated the powers of darkness and has placed His Spirit in every believer.

> *"You, however, are not in the flesh but in the Spirit, if in fact the Spirit of God dwells in you. Anyone who does not have the Spirit of Christ does not belong to him. But if Christ is in you, although the body is dead because of sin, the Spirit is life because of righteousness. If the Spirit of him who raised Jesus from the dead dwells in you, he who raised Christ Jesus from the dead will also give life to your mortal bodies through his Spirit who dwells in you."* (Romans 8:9–11, ESV)

Within every believer is the abundant power to overcome the pull of the flesh. Every believer has this indwelling power since every believer has the Spirit.

As a pastor, I do not know how many times I have heard people accusing other believers of not having the Spirit. Frankly I became sick of hearing people make this statement. It is a boldfaced lie and to propagate it is to do the bidding of the adversary to the detriment of the hearer. The truth is that every believer has the Spirit. They just need to be reminded of this fact and that the Spirit gives them the power to live in victory over the flesh. Paul wrote, *"But I say, walk by the Spirit, and you will not gratify the desires of the flesh"* (Galatians 5:16, ESV). It is absolutely possible for believers to live in victory over the power of their fleshly cravings. The issue is one of a believer's walk. This involves a conscious effort. It is an effort born in the heart of the believer that will result in prayerful self-examination and the subsequent drive to avoid being controlled by fleshly lusts. Every believer has a personal responsibility in this. Paul specifically wrote regarding this issue.

> *"Therefore, my beloved, as you have always obeyed, so now, not only as in my presence but much more in my absence, work out your own salvation with fear and trembling, for it is God who works in you, both to will and to work for his good pleasure."* (Philippians 2:12–13, ESV)

Paul exhorted the Philippians to work at putting their saving faith to practice in every aspect of their daily lives. Their motivation for this was to please to God. Yet they also needed to understand that they could not accomplish this in their own strength. They were to realize that God was working in them by His Spirit, empowering them to be successful in this effort. In other words, God through saving grace creates a desire in all believers to live above the lusts of the flesh and works in them to provide the strength necessary for success in this effort.

Thus, the first essential step in developing the mind of Christ is an effort by the believer to do so. Without this nothing will happen. The second step is continual spiritual transformation.

Believers must experience ongoing spiritual transformation. – The second essential step in developing the mind of Christ is the continuous spiritual transformation of the believer through renewing of the mind. This involves the motivation of the believer, the ministry of the Holy Spirit, and the word of God. Regarding this work, Paul wrote the following to the Roman believers.

> *"I appeal to you therefore, brothers, by the mercies of God, to present your bodies as a living sacrifice, holy and acceptable to God, which is your spiritual worship. Do not be conformed to this world, but be transformed by the renewal of your mind, that by testing you may discern what is the will of God, what is good and acceptable and perfect."* (Romans 12:1–2, ESV)

This passage is a key transition from the theology Paul presented in his letter to the practical outworking of grace in the believer's life. Here, Paul presented two principals for spiritual growth and developing the mind of Christ.

First, believers must have a proper view of the mercies of God. – Paul reminded the believers of God's amazing grace and mercy. His appeal to be living sacrifices was not based upon human wisdom or effort. It was based upon all the undeserved blessings that God showered upon those who had believed. They were the recipients of infinite and undeserved blessings. God had forgiven them of every transgression, given them an eternal inheritance, made them partakers of the divine nature, and granted them more than can be expressed in this writing. Moreover, God provided eternal redemption. Even if they sinned after believing they were covered by the redemptive work of Christ on the cross (1 John 2:1-2).

Thus, if believers would truly reflect upon God's manifold blessings, they would naturally have the motivation to offer their lives to Him. Here Paul used an analogy that takes the reader back to the Jewish Tabernacle and the work of the priests. He wrote, *"present your bodies as a living sacrifice, holy and acceptable to God, which is your spiritual worship."* They were to be living sacrifices. This phrase deals with the heart of the believer. In the Tabernacle the priests would offer the sacrifices of animals to cover the sins committed by the people. The animal was slain, the blood drained, and the best portions burned on the altar. Yet a living sacrifice is something different. Being living sacrifices implies that believers will be giving up their own fleshly wants and desires continuously. In doing so they offer their lives to God and His will as a pleasing aroma rising for His glory.

In this offering of one's body as a living sacrifice, we have the connection to "*spiritual worship.*" This is an interesting phrase as it is the Greek *logiken latreian*. The word *logiken* refers to something rational and logical. It comes from *logos*, which refers to something said (Strong G3050, 3056). Remembering that what proceeds from the mouth comes from the heart (Matt 15:18), this worship is that which proceeds logically from the heart of one who has a reverent view of God's mercies. Moreover, the word *latreian* is one of many words translated as worship in the Bible. This particular word refers to divine service (Strong G2999). It ties into the picture of the work of the priests in the Tabernacle and refers to what believers do in their daily lives as an act of worship. Believers who offer themselves as living sacrifices practice a supreme act of worship to God.

Therefore, it is reasonable or logical that believers who have a proper view of God's mercies will be motivated to continuously offer themselves to God for His purposes and glory. This is the prime motivation necessary to experience continual spiritual transformation, which results in developing the mind of Christ.

Second, believers must avoid and engage. – In Romans 12:2, Paul presents the practical responses that believers must manifest to experience spiritual transformation. They are avoidance and engagement. While using these two words may appear as a logical contradiction, it is not. Believers are to continuously avoid one thing and engage with another.

<u>Believers must avoid being conformed to the standards of the world system</u>. Paul wrote, "*Do not be conformed to this world.*" When I was a teenager, I had a neighborhood friend. He was quite the neighborhood renegade. I was not, at least not until I became his

friend. He did not do extremely bad things but got into mischief in the neighborhood. He was that guy who irritated all the neighbors. I guess his parents thought that I might have a positive influence on him and I guess in some ways I did. However, he also had a negative influence on me. I began getting involved in some of the mischief that he enjoyed. The point is this. There are influences all around us that can affect us in negative ways. Just as this friend had a negative influence on me, this world system has a negative influence on us.

John wrote this exhortation regarding the influence of the world system.

> *"Do not love the world or the things in the world. If anyone loves the world, the love of the Father is not in him. For all that is in the world—the desires of the flesh and the desires of the eyes and pride of life—is not from the Father but is from the world. And the world is passing away along with its desires, but whoever does the will of God abides forever."* (1 John 2:15–17, ESV)

The world system is that program instituted by Satan, which is diametrically opposed to the purposes and ways of God. It includes the lusts of the flesh, the cravings for things that will control our lives if we are not careful. It includes the lusts of the eyes, the desire to bring pleasures into our minds by what we see. Many of the things we see can influence the desires of our hearts and take us away from the purposes and plans of God.

The largest thing the world system promotes is the pride of life. Pride is a killer. It may be the number one overriding problem of humanity. It started in the Garden of Eden as the devil tempted Eve to be like God through partaking from the tree of the knowledge of good and evil. Today, it is something with which even the most righteous person struggles. Those who say they do not struggle with pride are by their own admission helplessly bound by it.

We must avoid being conformed to this world system. The word *"conformed"* is a present tense imperative meaning it is a continuous command. Believers are commanded to continuously avoid the power of the world system that works to conform them to Satan's evil ways. The problem is that its influences are all around us and can subconsciously conform us by what we see, hear, and experience.

One of the primary ways we are being conformed to the image of this world is through the various forms of media. Studies have indicated that the average person watches about 141 hours of television per month and that older folks, 55-64 years of age, watch the most. Children are not far behind. Kids 8-12 years old spend 4-6 hours per day looking at a screen and teens up to 9 hours per day (Lake). These are alarming statistics when you consider what people are watching and its influence on them. What comes across the airwaves is filled with worldly philosophies.

In the early seventies, while pursuing a bachelor's degree, I took a class in communications. We discussed at length the influence that media had on shaping people's view on social and moral issues. In fact, we concluded that the long-term effect of television and other forms of media could modify cultural behavior. We looked at a prime example of this in WWII. The Nazi party in Germany used media propaganda to sway a nation into either accepting or turning a blind eye to their immoral national policies. These very policies resulted in national conquest and the genocide of millions of Jewish people.

From the study of examples like that of Nazi Germany and others, sociologists and psychologists have generally accepted that media plays a significant role on cultural attitudes and behaviors (Mass Media and Communication) (Understanding Media and Culture).

Basically, the media has an ability to modify behavior without one noticing it. While there are many theories as to how this happens, the general consensus is that it does. For example, a 2006 study done on the effects of exposure to sexual content in various forms of media concluded, "young people with heavy exposure to sexually themed media ranging from music to movies are twice as likely to engage in early sexual behavior as young people with light exposure" (Understanding Media and Culture 62). While media executives believe that they are just portraying the way life is today, we cannot deny that there is a rapid transformation of social values. It seems that there is a vicious cycle where the media and contemporary culture chase one another down a steady spiral of moral decline.

What is the solution? Unfortunately, we are not going to eliminate the world system and we are not going to eliminate the evils of media. This is not within our power. We know that a day is coming when the Lord will do this. Today we must work to guard ourselves from it. We can regulate what we see, read, and hear. Everyone has an on and off button on their television remote. We can spend more time as a family talking to one another and in particular of the things pertaining to the faith. However, just shutting off the negative influences of the world system is not enough. Believers need to take a step further.

<u>Believers must be continuously transformed by the renewing of the mind</u>. It is always important to look for alternatives or contrasts in the study of Scripture. Here we see the word "*but,*" which prefaces an alternative. Paul wrote, "*Do not be conformed to the pattern of this world, but.*" There is an alternative direction that believers must take. Rather than conformation there is to be transformation. Rather than an external force conforming believers there is to be an internal work transforming them.

The word translated "*transformation*" is the Greek verb *metamorphoo*, from which we get the word metamorphosis. The work of transformation is a process that is to occur in believers' lives. The best example we have is that of a caterpillar undergoing a metamorphosis in a cocoon and coming out as a butterfly. The picture is one of entering the process as a relatively ugly creature and emerging with beauty. This is the process into which every believer has entered by saving faith in Jesus Christ. The old person tainted by sin and fleshly desires enters the faith and begins a process of continuous transformation into Christlikeness. The process continues throughout every believer's earthly life and culminates when they enter eternal glory.

Yet in this process of spiritual transformation there is an active part in which the believer must engage. The verse tells us that believers are commanded to *"be transformed by the renewal of"* their minds. This renewal is dependent upon what information believers feed to their minds. What the believers read, see, and hear will directly influence their minds and this process of transformation. In the old computer programming days, our teacher used to tell us, "*Garbage in, garbage out.*" In other words, the result of our computer program was only as good as the program code we typed into it. In the process of spiritual transformation believers must immerse themselves into the truth of God's word. His word alone is completely true, perfect, and holy.

We must avoid being conformed by the world system and instead seek to have the Holy Spirit transform us through the intake of God's word, the Bible. We experience inner transformation in a supernatural way. It happens when we listen to good preaching and teaching of the word. It happens when we read and study the Scriptures. The more we immerse ourselves in God's word, the more we will develop the mind of Christ, which is the ability to understand Scripture and apply it in life. Therefore, it behooves every believer to devote as much time as possible into the intake of God's word.

The Blessing of developing the Mind of Christ.

All of this has a desired end. As we are being transformed and developing the mind of Christ, we will naturally experience something that every true believer wants. Paul stated it, *"but be transformed by the renewal of your mind, that by testing you may discern what is the will of God, what is good and acceptable and perfect."* We will gain the ability to *"discern what is the will of God."*

The word *"discern"* here, *dokimazo*, means to test, examine, and discern things (Strong G1381). As believers grow in this work of spiritual transformation, they will increase in their ability to critically examine the situations and choices that they encounter in life. Thus, they will be able to discern the best choices, which are those aligned with the will of God.

Having been a believer for over forty-years, I have seen some believers who just seem to have it all together. They encounter situations and just naturally understand how the Lord would have them respond. They are not panicking. They are not stressed. They exude the peace of God and great confidence. The difference between them and others is that they have matured. They are not yet perfect but they characteristically respond to situations in a godly way, more so than others. You will often hear these believers responding to a situation by quoting Scripture, reminding themselves of the biblical course of action and they take that course.

There is much peace in this. Every believer has the capacity to grow in the ability to examine and discern things from a biblical standpoint. However, it takes engaging in the word of God. The unfortunate thing in Corinth was that they were stunted in their spiritual growth. Thus, they did not have this ability. They evidenced being conformed to the pattern of the world rather than being transformed by the renewing of the mind. Thus, their actions were far from godliness. Yet they did not have to stay there and neither does any believer. God has given us everything we need to grow in Christ likeness. We must just step out by faith, seeking Him and His righteousness in His word.

Chapter 3 – Hearing the Voice of the Lord

"And after the earthquake a fire, but the Lord was not in the fire. And after the fire the sound of a low whisper." (1 Kings 19:12, ESV)

In my undergraduate engineering studies at college, I worked in a cooperative education program. The college had students work for six-months every year in a degree related field as part of the educational process. I worked at the United States Steel Corporation. In my first year I worked in the power plant. In this location there were two turbo-generators and several turbo-blowers. These made so much noise that it was difficult or near impossible to hear another person talking. We would have to shout in order to be heard, even when standing just a couple feet apart.

Noise is a great problem in communication because it prevents us from being able to hear properly. In fact, too much loud noise for too long can damage one's ability to hear. So, to hear a voice it often becomes essential to cut or filter out other conflicting noises.

We have the same problem when trying to hear from the Lord. Often the circumstances of our lives can produce a lot of noise that will hinder and perhaps block our ability to hear clearly from the Lord.

The Experience of Elijah the Prophet

We can learn much about hearing the voice of the Lord from an experience that Elijah the prophet had. Elijah was a prophet during the reign of King Ahab and Queen Jezebel of the Northern Kingdom, Israel. The problem was that the Israelites in the Northern Kingdom were engaged in the worship of the false god, Baal. Their devotion was divided between Baal and the one true

Steven B. Hankins, Th.D.

God of Israel. This incensed Elijah, a true prophet of God, and he called Israel to make a choice. *"How long will you go limping between two different opinions? If the Lord is God, follow him; but if Baal, then follow him"* (1 Kings 18:21, ESV).

To resolve this issue Elijah proposed a great contest with the 450 prophets of Baal on Mount Carmel. The contest would prove to the Israelites that there was only one true God, Israel's God. In that contest, Elijah had the prophets of Baal make an altar for the sacrifice of a bull and he also made one. He challenged the prophets of Baal to call upon their god, Baal, to bring down fire upon the altar and Elijah would call upon Israel's God to do the same. Whoever succeeded in this would win the contest and prove whether Baal or Israel's God was the true God.

The prophets of Baal built their altar from stones, placed wood upon it, and a bull that was slain. They called upon Baal from morning until noon and nothing happened. Then they began cutting themselves and raving. At twilight, having failed to call down fire on their altar, it was Elijah's turn.

Elijah built an altar, piled wood upon it, and the bull that was slain. He made a trench around the altar and had the altar, the wood, and the bull saturated with water twice over. Then he called upon the Lord God to bring fire down. The Scripture states that immediately that is what happened.

> *"the fire of the Lord fell and consumed the burnt offering and the wood and the stones and the dust, and licked up the water that was in the trench"* (1 Kings 18:38, ESV).

Yes, the fire that came down was so intense that it consumed everything including the stones and the dust. Israel's God, the God of Abraham, Isaac, and Jacob, the Creator of all, was the one true God.

The victory was undeniable. *"And when all the people saw it, they fell on their faces and said, 'The Lord, he is God; the Lord, he is God'"* (1 Kings 18:39, ESV). The Israelites responded with reverence and confessed that the Lord was God. This implied that they would no longer be divided between opinions. They would follow the Lord God of Israel. Elijah then called upon Israel to seize the 450 prophets of Baal and he put them to death by the sword.

Next Elijah prayed to end a three-and one-half-year drought. After this he ran ahead of Ahab's chariot to Jezreel. There Ahab told Jezebel everything that happened on Mount Carmel. Upon hearing this she sent word to Elijah that she would have him killed just as he had the prophets of Baal killed. Elijah then fled for his life to Beersheba in the Southern Kingdom, Judah. He went another day's journey into the wilderness where he sat under a tree. Feeling like a failure and in a state of depression, he asked that he might die. Yet there he rested and the angel of the Lord ministered to him with food and water so that he would gain his strength. This he needed for the forty day and night journey to Mount Horeb. When he arrived at the mount, he entered a cave where he heard from the Lord. In this cave experience we will see two principles vital to hearing the voice of the Lord, stillness and sensitivity.

To hear from the Lord, we need stillness.

Elijah had experienced a great victory for the Lord. He was on the high of highs. Yet we see something happen to him. In fleeing from Jezebel's threats, he went from the high of highs to the low of lows. As a result, his life became filled with noise. He was physically and emotionally spent. Elijah needed a break. He needed stillness. James tells us that *"Elijah was a man with a nature like ours"* (James 5:17, ESV). All people struggle with the same human frailties that Elijah did and with them the noise that hinders our ability to hear from the Lord. The solution is to identify the sources of noise in our lives, do our best to eliminate them, and then experience stillness before the Lord so that we can hear from Him.

Understand the sources of noise that hinder our ability to hear. – When we look at Elijah, we see a man exhausted both physically and emotionally. We often find ourselves caught up in the busyness of life and, just like him, become physically and emotionally exhausted. In these times we can lose our focus and our capability to properly hear and process the word of the Lord. In our life's activity, exhaustion and uncontrolled emotions are usually connected. These sources of noise can hinder and even block us from hearing the Lord's voice. This produces a struggle in discerning our thoughts and ideas to see if they conform with God's will. There are four major types of noise that we experience in our lives every day. The first step in experiencing the stillness needed to hear from the Lord is to understand these various sources of noise.

Emotional Noise - Elijah typified a person filled with emotional noise as he was running from Queen Jezebel's death threat. Sometimes emotion so fills us that we do not focus on the Lord. We struggle with fear, anxiety, depression, and a host of other things. The problem is that we end up focusing more on the problem than the Lord who is our solution.

Many times, when I have found myself in a crisis, I fretted so much about the crisis that I forgot to seek the Lord for a solution. Often the last thing we do is call upon the Lord and sit quietly listening for the truth of Scripture that will quiet the soul. Yet when we do take time to pray and seek the Lord, we will experience the peace of God which transcends all understanding (Phil 4:6-7). It is when we find this rest in Him that He will reveal a much better way to negotiate the issue at hand (James 1:5).

I remember a time when I was demoted from a prominent position as the Plant Manager in a manufacturing operation. I honestly felt abused by my boss and the company. Yes, I was bitter. I knew it was wrong to feel that way but I could not shake it. That Saturday I sat down in my living room harboring all the bitterness and I began to pray for the Lord to take away the bitter emotion I was harboring. During the prayer the Lord reminded me of several facts. First, that He was always with me and had never left. Second, that He understood what went on, how hard I worked, and that I was taking all the right steps in the job. Last, He made me understand that the only thing that mattered was how He saw the situation. After hearing this I had immediate peace. Unfortunately, a couple hours later I allowed bitterness into my heart again. So, I went through the same process of prayer and received the same answer. I ended up repeating this process three or four times and then on Sunday afternoon, by God's grace, the bitterness left me for good. I returned to the plant on Monday morning without the bitterness and had an ability to work with my boss in a genuinely harmonious way.

We all experience times of emotional struggle. We need to recognize these emotions and how their control over us hinders our ability to hear from the Lord. The solution is to seek the Lord and the promises of His word. When we do, we will experience the peace and stillness necessary to hear from Him.

Busyness – Sometimes we are just too busy. Elijah was on the run. Generally, while you are running you are not thinking deeply. We, like Elijah, run too much from one thing to the next. We need to stop running so we can properly focus on God.

One time I was working on a printing press in Minnesota that had a significant problem. I spent an entire day troubleshooting the machine only to have it worse off at the end of the day than when I started. I was distraught. That night I called my wife from the hotel. She could hear how discouraged I was. She asked me one poignant question, "Have you read your Bible and prayed?" Wow, did that one hurt! Yet she was right. As we got off the phone, I opened the Gideon placed Bible in the hotel room and went to the helps in time of need section. It pointed me to Proverbs 3:5-6. It was just what I needed.

> *"Trust in the Lord with all your heart, and do not lean on your own understanding. In all your ways acknowledge him, and he will make straight your paths"* (Proverbs 3:5–6, ESV).

I purposed in my heart to trust the Lord in this and acknowledge Him in my work.

At 7:00am the next morning I went to the plant with only a vague idea of what to do. As soon as I opened the door to the plant the solution came to me. I knew exactly what the problem was. The plant maintenance representative was waiting at the door and I told him, "I know what is wrong. The Lord gave me insight." That morning I calmly and systematically worked through two major issues on the machine. The day before I was so frantically looking at things that I did not take time with the Lord. I truly believe that the Lord gave me insight to the problem that was formerly clouded by my busyness in trying to get the machine fixed.

Priorities – One large area of noise is the misdirected priorities of life. This is where everything but the Lord ends up being our priority. Elijah was worried about his own life and lost sight of the Lord and His purposes. Often, we allow our own wants and desires to gain top priority rather than the things of God. It is so easy to become distracted from what really matters. Our hobbies, entertainment, work, and a host of other things can become our number one priority and we can miss the mark.

Years ago, I went to an Evangelism Explosion Teacher Training Course in Omaha Nebraska. There I stayed with a young couple during the training. In the evenings, when I got back to their house, we had some great conversations. In one of those the couple indicated that at one time they were into softball but to them softball became sin. I was puzzled by their statement and asked why they felt this way. They told me that what started out as something fun, softball, had soon consumed their lives. They started missing their Wednesday evening corporate prayer time. They ceased with their daily devotional time. Ultimately, the schedule even interrupted their Sunday morning corporate worship times. They skipped church. Finally, they concluded that they needed to quit softball and devote themselves to the Lord anew. It was not that softball was sin but that softball had caused them to sin by getting their priorities out of order. They committed a sin of omission. James wrote, "*So whoever knows the right thing to do and fails to do it, for him it is sin"* (James 4:17, ESV). They had ceased doing the things that they knew the Lord wanted them to do

Our priorities in life can easily get out of order. We need to reevaluate the priorities of our lives frequently. Are my priorities in the correct order? What things are taking me away from that which is the most important? It will require repentance leading to a reprioritization of life to eliminate this noise.

Idolatry – Similar to the experience the couple in Omaha Nebraska described, idolatry can become a significant noise that keeps us from hearing from the Lord. The couple, due to misplaced priorities had turned softball, a good thing, into an idol. Oh, they did not worship softball in the way we normally see idolatry in the Bible but an idol is anything that steals our priority of devotion to God.

How can idolatry create noise in our lives? The problem is that it can adversely affect our ability to trust the Lord. When we struggle to trust the Lord, we do not readily seek His wisdom. While Elijah was running in the wilderness, he only sought the Lord to have his life ended. He did not seek for direction. It happens to all of us. Yet if we are not trusting in the Lord, we are trusting something else. Anything we trust other than the Lord is a form of idolatry. There are many things that can become idols to us. Some that even seem as though they are not.

As a pastor I have often been caught in the trap of trusting that some program or thing would cause the ministry to flourish. In my last church we went through a host of ministries and programs. Many of these were models derived by other successful churches. Without any significant prayer we implemented these things believing that they would make the church prosper. We were very foolish in this. We needed to realize that only the Lord builds the church (Matt 16:18) and this meant trusting Him. The most successful ministries we started were not copied verbatim from other churches but established after long times of prayer. Understand that anything can become an idol if we are not careful.

Idols will produce significant noise in our lives that will keep us from hearing the Lord's voice.

We must eliminate the noise of life so we can hear from the Lord. – While there is so much noise in life, there also is hope. By God's grace we can eliminate the noise and experience stillness so that we can hear from the Lord. We can learn much in this regard from Elijah's experience as he came to a cave.

> *"There he came to a cave and lodged in it. And behold, the word of the Lord came to him, and he said to him, "What are you doing here, Elijah?" He said, "I have been very jealous for the Lord, the God of hosts. For the people of Israel have forsaken your covenant, thrown down your altars, and killed your prophets with the sword, and I, even I only, am left, and they seek my life, to take it away."* (1 Kings 19:9–10, ESV)

Once we visited a place called "Mammoth Cave," which was a limestone cavern. We went down inside the cave with a guide and saw the limestone formations, the stalagmites, and stalactites. While in the cave the guide wanted us to see the cave in its natural lighting. So, he turned off his flashlight and shut off all the lights. Regardless of how hard you strained your eyes you could not see a thing. Moreover, everyone remained silent and you could hear a pin drop. In the cave there were no distractions, nothing to see and nothing to hear. It was a place where you would notice anything unusual. This is the setting in which we find Elijah after his flight from Jezebel and arriving at Mt. Horeb. He found himself in a cave, a quiet place, a place where he could quiet the noise of life.

While most of us do not have a limestone cavern in our backyard, we still need to eliminate the noise that prevents us from hearing the Lord's voice. Elijah's experience reveals several practical ways to eliminate noise from our lives so we can hear clearly from the Lord.

Find Time for Solitude – We must devote time for solitude. Elijah came to the cave where he stopped and entered a period of solitude. He was all alone. There were no outside distractions. He had nothing to do. He had no smart phone, no television, and no one to interrupt him. There he could quiet his life and hear from the Lord. We see other examples of this in the Scriptures. The Gospels record that Jesus took four retreats with His disciples. These were times for Him and the disciples to get away from the busyness of ministry for rest, prayer, and instruction. Scripture tells us that even Jesus needed quiet time with the Father as Luke recorded, *"Jesus often withdrew to lonely places and prayed"* (Luke 5:16, ESV). If Jesus, God the Son, needed solitude and time to speak with the Father, how much more do we need the same. This is a model that every believer must follow.

As previously mentioned, our lives are full of distractions. Sometimes I get so busy writing that I forget to get quiet with the Lord. We see a prime example of this when Jesus went to Mary and Martha's home and Martha was busy preparing a meal for the occasion. In the record of the visit, we see that Mary sat at Jesus' feet and listened to Him while *"Martha was distracted with much serving"* (Luke 10:40a, ESV). The word distracted, *perispao*, literally means to be dragged all about (Strong G4049). Her busyness dragged her all about and literally prevented her from taking in what the Lord had to say.

Martha then complained to the Lord about Mary, *"Lord, do you not care that my sister has left me to serve alone? Tell her then to help me"* (Luke 10:40b, ESV). See how Jesus responded to her.

> *"Martha, Martha, you are anxious and troubled about many things, but one thing is necessary. Mary has chosen the good portion, which will not be taken away from her"* (Luke 10:41–42, ESV).

Mary was alone with Jesus. She was focused on hearing what Jesus had to say. However, Martha's busyness distracted her from being able to hear the voice of the Lord.

We all must find a time to be alone with the Lord. Some time ago, I was struggling with the thought of retiring from the pastorate. I knew it was time to bring a younger pastor into the church but I was struggling emotionally with this transition. In a moment of crisis, I drove to the beach and sat on some rocks all by myself and stared out to the horizon. It was there that the Lord brought me to a place of peace and direction. We all need alone times with Jesus.

Find a Tranquil Place – To experience solitude, we must find a quiet place, one that is away from the noise. Elijah found a cave, a place of solitude. I previously mentioned visiting "Mammoth Cave" and experiencing its solitude. It was a quiet place, one in which a person could get away from the distractions of life. We all need a quiet place. Consider your house or office. Phones will ring. People will barge in. Dogs will bark and alert you to something outside. The kids will want attention. The television is blaring. I think you get the picture. How can you spend time listening to the Lord amid such chaos? I guess it may be possible but it is not easy. Not many of us have a cave in our backyard but we all must find a quiet tranquil place. It might be a room in your home after you put the children to bed where there are no other distractions. It might be the place in the park or the woods behind your house. It might be that secluded place at the beach. One thing is certain. You can find a place of solitude if you just look for it.

In the movie "Sargent York" there is a scene where York is trying to determine what he should do regarding military service. He is torn regarding his biblical convictions against killing and serving his country. There was a special place where he would go on the side of a mountain to commune with the Lord on serious matters. It was a quiet tranquil place. There he spent time in prayer and searched the word of God for an answer. In that quiet tranquil place of solitude, he received the direction he needed from the Lord.

The place where we will hear from God is normally a quiet tranquil place. It will be a lonely place where it is just you and the Lord. It will be a reflective place where you can meditate on the things of God. All of us must find such a place and spend time with the Lord there.

To hear from the Lord, we need sensitivity.

Once we find the quiet place, we need to have a heart that is sensitive to the Lord's leading. Previously I mentioned attending an Evangelism Explosion Teacher Training Conference with the pastor of the church I joined. It was about six-months after the Lord saved me. I was in a conference with about 200 pastors and missionaries. At that time a new Bible translation had been recently published, the New International Version, NIV. Prior to attending the conference, I went to the bookstore and purchased a genuine leather-bound NIV pocket Testament. At the conference I met a missionary who saw it and asked me where I got it. He was looking for one prior to going back on the mission field. After hearing this I gave the one I had to him. When my pastor found out he made a comment that struck me. He said that he had never seen a young believer who was so sensitive to the leading of the Holy Spirit. I did not fully understand what he was saying at the time but sensitivity is essential when it comes to hearing the voice of the Lord.

What Elijah experienced in the cave shows us something about the sensitivity needed to hear the voice of the Lord.

> *"And he said, 'Go out and stand on the mount before the Lord.' And behold, the Lord passed by, and a great and strong wind tore the mountains and broke in pieces the rocks before the Lord, but the Lord was not in the wind. And after the wind an earthquake, but the Lord was not in the earthquake. And after the earthquake a fire, but the Lord was not in the fire. And after the fire the sound of a low whisper."*
> (1 Kings 19:11–12, ESV)

This is an interesting segment in the story. We see the Lord speaking with Elijah and then telling him to go out and stand on the mount before the Lord. Here we see some ways with which the Lord will communicate with us. Some ways require greater sensitivity than others.

Ways of Communication – The Lord communicates with us in a variety of ways. At times He speaks to us through the grandiose. However, most often He speaks to us through the soft and subtle.

In my life I have experienced some loud talkers and some who barely whisper. Sometimes in a restaurant you will hear a table of loud people talking. Their voices are unmistakable and discernable. When I am there, I will often be inclined to shout out, "Inside voice please." However, being a Christian I understand that they do not realize what they are doing and forgive. Yet there are others who speak so softly that you can barely hear them even when they are right in front of you. To hear these, we need a quiet place and an attentive ear. It is the same with the Lord. Sometimes He speaks loudly through the grandiose and other at times He speaks through the "*sound of a low whisper.*" The King James Version translates this as a "*still small voice*" (1 Kings 19:12, KJV). When the Lord speaks in this "*still small voice*" the believer needs to be very attentive.

Through the Grandiose — Elijah stood in the mouth of the cave and the Lord passed by. There are three grandiose manifestations: a wind that tears a mountain, an earthquake, and a fire. Yet Elijah does not hear from the Lord in these. While Elijah did not hear the from the Lord in these, there are times when the Lord does speak through the grandiose, the miraculous, that is the loud voice. This normally happens when there is an imminent situation in which He needs to get our attention immediately.

Imagine someone is in front of you and not paying attention to where he is going. You might softly say, "Hey watch where you are going." However, if you see they are about to walk in front of a moving bus your voice will change. You will yell loudly, "Watch out! Stop!" These are two types of situations and two voice levels. It is that way when the Lord speaks to us. The Lord will speak loudly when his children are about to walk from the path of righteousness to a dangerous path of sin. The voice may be like this, "Don't take that. It is stealing!" "Don't cheat on your taxes!" Sometimes it may be, "You are on the wrong path! Repent!" Here,

I am speaking of that inner conviction that happens when we may be tempted to walk off the path of righteousness.

Moreover, there are also times when the Lord uses the providential circumstances of life to get our attention. It may be a financial crisis, an illness, a relationship issue, some world event, etc. These grandiose events will often cause us to refocus on our relationship with the Lord. They will bring us to seek wisdom from the Lord. In the context of trials James wrote, *"If any of you lacks wisdom, let him ask God, who gives generously to all without reproach, and it will be given him"* (James 1:5, ESV). In these times we will be drawn to seek the Lord and His wisdom.

Through the Soft and Subtle – However, normally the Lord speaks to us in a *"still small voice,"* the soft and subtle. This happens when we seek Him in His word. Elijah did not experience the Lord in the three grandiose manifestations. However, when he heard the *"still small voice"* he knew that it was the Lord and he responded. While the Lord does speak through the grandiose, He normally speaks to us in a soft and subtle way, especially when we are seeking Him for direction in life or answers to specific issues.

In the cave, Elijah had a very specific issue with which he was dealing. He was perplexed and needed an answer that would settle his soul.

> *"What are you doing here, Elijah?" He said, "I have been very jealous for the Lord, the God of hosts. For the people of Israel have forsaken your covenant, thrown down your altars, and killed your prophets with the sword, and I, even I only, am left, and they seek my life, to take it away."* (1 Kings 19:9–10, ESV)

Elijah was in a state of distress. He felt like he was left all alone, the lone surviving prophet and true follower of God. He seemed uncertain about his future and he did not know what to do. Can you sense his frustration? It is the answer to this dilemma that he hears through the *"still small voice."*

When we are looking for answers in life, we need to hear that *"still small voice."* It comes as we meet the Lord in a tranquil place apart from the noise of life. It is when we commune with Him in prayer through His word. As we sit, pray, read, and study the Bible, we will gain insight from God through His word. This insight comes in our thoughts via the *"still small voice."* In these times of prayer and contemplation of the word of God, He by the ministry of the Holy Spirit applies the truth of the Scriptures to our hearts. In this we gain insight in applying God's truth to our specific situations.

Recognizing the Voice – How do we know if we have heard from the Lord on an issue? Well, this is what "The Seven Filters" is about. For now, just understand this fact. When we hear the voice of the Lord, we will know for certain it is from Him and respond accordingly. When Elijah heard the *"still small voice"* he immediately recognized it as the Lord speaking.

> *"And when Elijah heard it, he wrapped his face in his cloak and went out and stood at the entrance of the cave. And behold, there came a voice to him and said, "What are you doing here, Elijah?"* (1 Kings 19:13, ESV)

He wrapped his cloak around his face as an expression of his reverence and responded by going to the entrance of the cave. Somehow, he knew that this *"still small voice"* was from the Lord. How was this different?

It is Recognizable – Elijah's action of wrapping his face with his cloak indicates that he clearly understood that the Lord was in the sound. When the people of God hear the *"still small voice,"* they will recognize that it is the voice of the Lord. Then having the assurance that it is the Lord speaking they will respond with reverence.

It is Personal – The Lord calls Elijah by name. This was a message specifically meant for Elijah. The Lord intends to speak to each one of us directly. He desires to give us the direction we need to fulfill our part in His great mission. At the mouth of the cave the Lord asked Elijah again, *"What are you doing here, Elijah?"* Elijah responded with what was on his heart. Then the Lord proceeded to give Elijah specific instructions regarding what he was to do and how the Lord was working in this. *"And the Lord said to him, 'Go, return on your way to the wilderness of Damascus'"* (1 Kings 19:15, ESV). The Lord still had plans for Elijah. He was not done with his service as a prophet. Elijah was to anoint men as kings and anoint Elisha as his replacement (1 Kings 19:15-16). Moreover, He told Elijah that the Lord had a remnant of 7,000 that had not bowed their knees to Baal (1 kings 19:18). He was not alone and God was still at work.

Many times, we will need direction from the Lord in life. I remember a time of discouragement in the ministry. Things were just not going well. I had experienced some rebellion from a couple of leaders in the church and it really hurt. I asked the pastors of the association to pray for me at one of the Friday pastors' prayer times. On Monday morning, as I was in my quiet place, my home office, reading the Scripture and praying, a verse of Scripture jumped out at me. It was the account of Joseph speaking to his brothers after their father Jacob had died. They were afraid of retaliation for what they had done to their brother. However, he responded to them with assurance.

> *"As for you, you meant evil against me, but God meant it for good, to bring it about that many people should be kept alive, as they are today"* (Genesis 50:20, ESV).

Through this verse *"the still small voice"* encouraged me to realize that the struggles I was experiencing in the church had a future purpose. It was that many more people could be reached with the hope of the gospel.

It is Clear and Discernable – When the Lord speaks, it is always clear and discernable. The Lord gave Elijah the clear and specific instructions necessary to fulfill his mission in God's providential program. As we examine what God told Elijah to do, we can see that Elijah responded with appropriate action. Elijah did anoint Elisha as his replacement and through Elisha the two kings were anointed (2 Kings 8:7-14; 9:1-3).

One of the seven filters that we will examine deals with the area of confusion. The Lord God will never lead us into confusion. He will always give clear direction to His children. *"For God is not a God of confusion but of peace"* (1 Corinthians 14:33, ESV). The Lord's communications are always clear and direct. He never leads one of His children astray. If what you hear is confusing or contradictory to Scripture, do not act upon it. In this case continue to seek affirmation from the Lord until you have clarity.

When I was saved in 1983, I had a bit of a crisis. Everything in my life changed. My desires and focus of life were completely different. Yet I was working with a group of people on a machine start-up in Minneapolis Minnesota who had a complete opposite philosophy of life. Of course, prior to my conversion I was right there with them. I would sit with them at lunch and laugh-it-up as I listened to their obscene jokes and talk. However, now I could not. This same stuff now seemed offensive to me. I frankly did not know how to handle this transition.

Every Friday evening, I would fly out of the Minneapolis Airport back to Chicago to go home. On the flight to Chicago, I was praying about my dilemma. I thought, should I quit my job to avoid the stuff that now seemed so repulsive? After landing in the O'Hare Airport, deplaning, and while walking through the terminal, I heard something. At least it seemed that way. A thought came to me that was so loud I thought it was an audible voice. I looked around and did not see anyone that could have made this voice in my head. The voice said, "Love all mankind." It was a loud voice I heard that evening in the Chicago O'Hare Airport.

As I considered this thought a couple verses of Scripture came to mind.

The Seven Filters

"For God so loved the world, that he gave his only Son, that whoever believes in him should not perish but have eternal life" (John 3:16, ESV).

After this I thought of the Great Commission. Through these verses came the understanding that I was not supposed to ignore these guys at the plant. Instead, I was to love them. Moreover, the most loving thing I could do was to share the joy of salvation with them. It would mean putting myself in an uncomfortable position, one with some risk. Yet this was a necessary one if I was to witness to them.

As I think back to this experience, I realize that I heard a loud voice in that airport. However, the understanding of what I was supposed to do came through the *"still small voice"* of the Lord speaking through the Scriptures. This is the only time I remember hearing such a loud voice from the Lord. You see, God normally imparts truth to us through the *"still small voice."* It takes much more sensitivity to hear the *"whisper"* of God but it is possible.

Every believer can hear the voice of the Lord and He does want to speak to us. However, there is a problem. We are dull of hearing. The noise of the world impairs our ability to hear. This noise comes in the way of unchecked emotions, busyness, misdirected priorities, and idolatry. To counter the noise, we need to find a quiet place, a place where we can focus on the Lord. We must realize that this quiet place is necessary because the Lord normally speaks in the *"still small voice."*

We all need quiet time with the Lord. I often need to get away from everything to have this. I will find a quiet place where I can pray, read the Scriptures, and seek the Lord's guidance through them as they apply to the issues of life. When I do this, I generally get clear thought and direction from the Lord. I will write down the thoughts or ideas that I have and then run them through the *"seven filters"* to make sure these things are from the Lord.

The next section of this book contains *"seven filters."* Perhaps now I have given many just enough information to be dangerous.

Not every thought or idea is from the Lord. The "*seven filters*" in the next section will present a systematic way to filter out the voices that are not from God.

Before you move on let me give two very important thoughts regarding the voice of the Lord. First, the Lord primarily speaks to us through His word, the Bible, as illuminated by the Holy Spirit. Second, if you think something is from the Lord but are not sure, do not act until you are certain. I will cover this again as we go through "The Seven Filters."

Section 2 – The Seven Filters

In our lives we have numerous thoughts every day. Some of these are good, some are bad, and some are neutral. Moreover, some of the thoughts will align with God's will for us and some may not.

Some of these thoughts are planted in our mind by the Holy Spirit in order to guide us in the purposes of God in life. However, there are other sources that plant thoughts in our minds. Sometimes our fleshly desires, other people, and spiritual forces opposed to the will of God can give us ideas that can get us off track with the will of God.

Section 2, "The Seven Filters," presents seven filters for discerning our thoughts to ensure our decision align with the will of God.

Filter #1 – Am I living like a spiritual person? ………….. 46

Filter #2 – Does the Bible say it is ok? ………………… 62

Filter #3 – Are my methods correct? …………………... 78

Filter #4 – Does it take true faith? …………………..… 91

Filter #5 – What do other spiritual people think? ………. 100

Filter #6 – Is my motive to glorify God alone? ………….122

Filter #7 – Am I absolutely certain? ……………..……..144

Steven B. Hankins, Th.D.

Filter #1 – Am I living like a spiritual person?

"The spiritual person judges all things, but is himself to be judged by no one."
(1 Corinthians 2:15, ESV)

I was commissioned into the United States Army as a Second Lieutenant in 1974. To prepare myself for service as an officer I purchased a book titled the "Officer's Guide." This guide is still published for use by Army officers today. It contains information that is designed to ensure that officers would look and act in accordance with their important position.

However, there were unfortunate times when officers did not reflect the high standards expected of them. In these cases, there were often breakdowns in the command structure, unit performance, the reputation of the officer, and potentially their units. When this happened, superior officers would take action to remedy the deficiencies in their subordinate officers. This was necessary to ensure that officers would always reflect highly upon the United States and the Army.

There is a similarity in the walk of a believer in Jesus. By faith the believer has become a spiritual person and the conduct of believers should reflect their blessed position as citizens of heaven and members of God's family. Yet sometimes believers do not act like the spiritual people that God has made them. In these cases, the believer's ability to walk in victory is significantly diminished. Accordingly, the believer's ability to hear and respond to the voice of the Lord is hindered. Every believer must live like a spiritual person should.

The Ability to Filter Out Noisy Thoughts.

Every day we have a plethora of thoughts and ideas. These prompt us to do the things we do. According to a study from Queen's University in Canada the average person has more than 6,000 thoughts in a day (Craig 7/13/2020). The problem with our thoughts is that they come from a variety of places. Many will come from our own fleshly desires. Others come from the external influences of the world system. Still more can come from demonic deceptions. And yes, some do come from godly influences that are aligned with the purposes and plans of God. So, some of the thoughts we have are good, some are bad, and many are morally neutral.

With all these thoughts it is imperative that believers filter them to ensure that they do not let things outside of the will of God influence their actions. The Scriptures state that believers are to *"take every thought captive to obey Christ"* (2 Corinthians 10:5, ESV). Only believers who are living like spiritual people will be able to successfully filter out the bad thoughts from the good.

Paul wrote to the Corinthians stating, *"The spiritual person judges all things."* The verb *"judges,"* *anakrino*, refers to an ability to scrutinize things (Strong G350). Spiritual people have the unique ability to examine every thought critically and comprehensively in every situation. In doing so they can filter out the bad and allow the good thoughts to direct their actions. Yet this ability to filter out the bad from the good only works if believers live like the spiritual people that God has made them. Therefore, there is one vital question that believers must ask when trying to determine if their thoughts are aligned with the will of God. **"Am I Living Like a Spiritual Person?"**

Someone once decided to make some morning coffee. However, he did not get the coffee filter in the machine correctly. After the coffee brewed, he discovered that there were grounds in the coffee. This made the finished coffee less than pleasant to drink. It is this way with our thoughts. We need to have the filter in place that will remove that which is unwanted from our thinking processes. This is so we will only act upon the thoughts that align with the will of God. The primary filter for removing the believer's bad thoughts is that of living like a spiritual person.

This first and most important filter has to do with the heart of the believer. To apply this filter the believer needs to ask this question honestly and prayerfully. "Am I living like a spiritual person?" If believers are not, they cannot trust their thoughts or ideas. This was the question at the heart of Paul's exhortation to the church in Corinth.

> *"But I, brothers, could not address you as spiritual people, but as people of the flesh, as infants in Christ. I fed you with milk, not solid food, for you were not ready for it. And even now you are not yet ready, for you are still of the flesh. For while there is jealousy and strife among you, are you not of the flesh and behaving only in a human way?"* (1 Corinthians 3:1–3, ESV)

The believers in Corinth had a drastic flaw in their character. The evidence of this was strife and jealousy between members of their congregation. This was because they were living by the flesh and not the Spirit. To better understand what it means to be living like a spiritual person let us first look at what a spiritual person is not and then what one is.

What the spiritual person is not.

Looking at the church in Corinth we see a picture of believers who are not acting like the spiritual people the Lord desires. The basis of our self-examination will first be to identify the flaws in our own hearts. There are certain characteristics that will identify what a spiritual person is not.

The spiritual person is not an unsaved person. – In Paul's letter to the Corinthians he wrote the following vital truth.

> *"The natural person does not accept the things of the Spirit of God, for they are folly to him, and he is not able to understand them because they are spiritually discerned."* (1 Corinthians 2:14, ESV)

In the context of this verse Paul explained that only the Spirit of God can understand the things of God (1 Cor 2:10-13). Thus, the natural man who cannot understand the things of God is the man void of the Spirit. The man void of the Spirit is one who is unsaved. We know this because Scripture clearly teaches us that every true believer is indwelt by the Spirit of God at the moment of salvation. (See Paul's clarification of this truth in Romans 8:9.)

Those without the Spirit are spiritually deaf. They cannot truly hear the voice of God because they have never heard and responded to the call of salvation. They have never trusted in the finished work of Christ through which one must be saved. Therefore, they do not receive the things of the Spirit and neither do they understand them. The word Paul used here for understand is *ginosko*. It refers to a knowledge that one gains through experience (Thayer p35). Since unsaved people have had no experience with Christ, they cannot understand the things of God.

The spiritual person is not a fleshly driven person. – In 1 Corinthians 3:1, Paul addressed those in Corinth as *"brothers,"* *adelphoi*. It is a term that refers to those of a common ancestry. Here Paul was not speaking about common ancestors from the same earthly parents. He used this term to refer to those who had the same heavenly parentage. Paul was addressing believers who by faith received Jesus and became children of God (John 1:12). Yet these believers were not acting like spiritual people. Instead, they were acting like little helpless children, *"infants in Christ."* The symptoms of this were that they exhibited jealousy and strife between one another (1 Cor 3:3-4).

Paul explained that *"infants in Christ"* are fleshly people. The word for infant, *nepios*, refers to one who is a babe in knowledge, unlearned, or simple (Thayer p123). This person is a believer but who still acts as an infant in the faith. This acting as an infant is not restricted to those who have just professed faith in Christ. Some have been in the faith for years but never progressed beyond childish things. Paul indicated that there are two flaws with these people.

Infants in Christ are flawed in their understanding. – Paul explained that these people are on milk rather than solid food. The writer of Hebrews echoed this same thought (Heb 5:11-14). They had not adequately grasped the basic tenets of the faith and needed the same things explained repeatedly. Thus, they had not matured sufficiently to move to solid food.

When we consider those who are flawed in their understanding, we will generally see two diverse problems. Some will be prone to legalism and seek to follow external rules and regulations. Others will be very liberal, believing that they can do whatever they want and it is ok. One of these types of deficiencies usually exist in the lives of believers who are *"infants in Christ."* This is because they have not progressed to a point where they know what it means to live by the Spirit (Gal 5:16).

Infants in Christ are flawed in their actions. – Paul explained that the Corinthians behaved in a human way. This was characterized by jealousy and strife as they established factions based upon their favorite teachers (1 Cor 3:3-4). Fleshly people, the spiritual infants, frequently allow certain characteristics of the flesh to control their lives. Thus, they act in a childish way regarding the faith.

Anyone who has had children understands the picture that Paul painted here. There is a phase in childhood development that we call *"the terrible twos."* It is that period in development where the child already has begun to understand parental instruction and exhortation but still does not hearken to it. When our daughter was at this stage my wife told her not to touch the stove. What did she do? You guessed it, she touched the stove. She understood mom's command but chose to disobey. While she did understand the word *"no,"* she would constantly disregard the warning. This is childish behavior. She was not ready to move onto more advanced things like how to cook or use an oven because she still did not understand what it meant to heed warnings. Immature and childish believers are like this. They need basic things repeated and are unable to progress because of fleshly behaviors.

From this we conclude that spiritual people are those genuinely saved by faith in Christ. We also understand that spiritual people do not let fleshly desires dominate their lives. Only spiritual people will consistently seek to discern their thoughts to determine if they are from God or their own human desires.

What the spiritual person is.

To determine if we are living like spiritual people, we must not just look for the negative but also the positives. In the Christian life if something is not positive it is negative. There is no neutral ground. It is this way with salvation and it is this way with living like a spiritual person. A person is either led by the Holy Spirit or led by the flesh. Paul explained this truth to the Galatians.

> *"But I say, walk by the Spirit, and you will not gratify the desires of the flesh. For the desires of the flesh are against the Spirit, and the desires of the Spirit are against the flesh, for these are opposed to each other, to keep you from doing the things you want to do."* (Galatians 5:16–17, ESV)

A person cannot follow the leading of both the flesh and the Spirit at the same time. Jesus presented this principle in the Sermon on the Mount.

> *"No one can serve two masters, for either he will hate the one and love the other, or he will be devoted to the one and despise the other. You cannot serve God and money"* (Matthew 6:24, ESV).

The old expression goes, "You cannot ride in two canoes at the same time." If you try it, you will eventually get soaked. So, what positive characteristics are present in one who lives like a spiritual person should?

The spiritual person evidences spiritual maturity. – In context of Paul's exhortation to the Corinthian church he indicated that the believer who is spiritual is one who is mature.

> *"Yet among the mature we do impart wisdom, although it is not a wisdom of this age or of the rulers of this age, who are doomed to pass away"* (1 Corinthians 2:6, ESV).

What is maturity? The word translated *"mature,"* teleios, has to do with something brought to its end or completion (Thayer p185-186). As this refers to a person it means fully-grown. Paul described a spiritually mature person in the book of Philippians. In the passage we see three characteristics of the spiritually mature person.

> *"Not that I have already obtained this or am already perfect, but I press on to make it my own, because Christ Jesus has made me his own. Brothers, I do not consider that I have made it my own. But one thing I do: forgetting what lies behind and straining forward to what lies ahead, I press on toward the goal for the prize of the upward call of God in Christ Jesus. Let those of us who are mature think this way, and if in anything you think otherwise, God will reveal that also to you."* (Philippians 3:12–15, ESV)

The spiritually mature person has a humble perspective. – Paul stated, *"Not that I have already obtained this or am already perfect"* (Philippians 3:12, ESV). Paul made this statement about himself. He realized that he had not already reached perfection. The verb translated *"perfect,"* teleioo, being in the perfect tense and passive voice is better understood this way, *"already been perfected."* The verb comes from the word, *teleios*, which is the word translated as *"mature"* in 1 Corinthians 2:6 and in Philippians 3:15. At the time of writing the Philippian letter Paul had been a believer for about 26 years, gone on three missionary journeys, and planted numerous churches. If anyone could claim the title of mature it would be Paul but he does not. Rather, he stated he has much more room for growth.

Paul further pointed out, "*Let those of us who are mature think this way.*" In other words, his point was that the mature person is a person who realizes he is not yet mature. The mature person is one who realizes that he still has a long way to go to reach the goal. Thus, this mature person is one who has a humble perspective.

Once I ran into a person who went to great lengths to tell me how mature he was. I had another who told me how humble he was. Neither of these people exemplified the humble attitude of Paul. The mature person is a humble person who realizes that he has a long way to go towards spiritual maturity.

The spiritually mature person has an intense desire for Christ-likeness. – From Paul's words, we can see that he had a strong desire and drive to be like Jesus.

> "*Brothers, I do not consider that I have made it my own. But one thing I do: forgetting what lies behind and straining forward to what lies ahead*" (Philippians 3:13, ESV).

The word Paul uses for "*straining forward,*" *epekteinomai*, means to stretch out towards something (Strong G1901). If you have ever watched a track and field event like an Olympic race you get an idea of this effort. Runners in a race will often get to the finish line and stretch out their upper bodies to cross the finish line ahead of the closest competitor. This gives us a good picture of what it means to have an intense desire for Christ-likeness. Believers should be stretching out in every possible way to reach the goal of spiritual maturity.

The spiritually mature person exerts tremendous effort to achieve the goal. In the passage, Paul stated that he pressed on toward the goal (Phil 3:14). This is the imagery of a person in a competitive race. It pictures the believer exerting much energy in running swiftly to pursue the goal. It implies the exertion of continuous effort to achieve the goal of Christ likeness. This type of person is engaged in a serious pursuit of the truth contained in the word of God with a desire to practice it in life.

The spiritual person is filled with the Spirit. – We know what a spiritual person looks like, but the question is this. How does a believer become a spiritual person who lives accordingly? It is a matter of being filled with the Spirit. Yet what does it mean to be filled with the Spirit?

One time I went to the gas station to fill up my container for the lawn-mower. I put my credit card in the slot on the pump, pushed the select grade button, took the hose out of the pump, and put it in my 5-gallon container. However, when I pulled the handle, nothing happened. I got a bit frustrated with the pump, cancelled the transaction, and tried again. The same thing happened. When I squeezed the pump handle nothing came out of the nozzle. Then the attendant came over and asked what was wrong. I said, "I can't get anything to come out of the nozzle." He said, "You are using the wrong nozzle." You see, there were two nozzles on the pump. One was green and the other black. Well, I was embarrassed. Yet the attendant saved me from making a big mistake.

When you go to a gas station to fill up your car you will often see a pump with two nozzles. One nozzle may have a green identification and the other various colors, most often black. The distinction is vital. The green nozzle indicates that it will pump diesel fuel. The black will pump out gasoline. If you pump diesel fuel into your gasoline-powered car you will quickly discover that your car will not run. Conversely, if you pump gasoline into a diesel-powered vehicle, you will damage the engine. It is a matter of what fuel you used to fill the tank.

This is a simple analogy but it should help us understand our spiritual lives. We are going to be filled with something. If it is not the Holy Spirit it is something else. Only by being filled with the Holy Spirit will our spiritual lives run correctly.

Today there is much confusion regarding the Holy Spirit's work of filling believers. Let us sort out the confusion and clearly understand this key doctrine. One of the key verses that presents the doctrine of being filled with the Spirit is in the book of Ephesians.

"And do not get drunk with wine, for that is debauchery, but be filled with the Spirit," (Ephesians 5:18, ESV)

There are several vital things that believers need to understand regarding being filled with the Spirit.

The Holy Spirit indwells every believer. – This has already been covered but since there is so much false teaching in this area it must be repeated. Paul wrote to the Romans that the Holy Spirit indwells every true believer in Jesus.

"You, however, are not in the flesh but in the Spirit, if in fact the Spirit of God dwells in you. Anyone who does not have the Spirit of Christ does not belong to him" (Romans 8:9, ESV).

Groups that say certain believers do not have the Spirit because they do not speak in tongues have not understood this verse and that it is by faith in Jesus Christ alone that one is saved (John 6:47; Eph 2:8-9). According to Romans 8:9 every believer in Jesus has received the indwelling presence of the Holy Spirit at the instant of saving faith. This universal indwelling of all believers began on the Day of Pentecost when the church was officially birthed (Acts 2). Thus, without exception every true believer has the Holy Spirit and the capacity to be filled with the Spirit. Yet not every believer who has the Holy Spirit is filled with the Spirit.

To be filled with the Spirit is to be controlled by the Spirit. – Every believer must consider this diagnostic question, "While I have all of the Spirit does the Spirit have all of me?" The big issue is one of control. You see, there is a difference between the indwelling presence of the Holy Spirit and the manifestation of the Holy Spirit in the believer.

When you look at Ephesians 5:18 you see two commands. The first one is in the negative, *"do not get drunk with wine."* When people get drunk, they are not in full control of their motor functions. We call drunk drivers *"impaired drivers"* for a reason. It is because their actions are not normal. People in this condition do not think straight. They often slur their speech and speak nonsense. They do not walk straight and they do not drive straight. Thus, the alcohol has taken control and modified their behavior.

We should look at this command to *"not get drunk with wine"* metaphorically. In others words, just as excessive alcohol can control a person's behavior other things of the world can do the same. Thus, believers cannot let anything of the world so fill their lives that those things will take control of their actions. These can be things that we normally consider good such as hobbies, sports, work, foods, etc. It can even include one's emotions, natural desires, relationships, etc.

The second command is in the positive, *"be filled with the Spirit."* This is a positive command. Since whatever fills our lives can lead and control us, we need to be filled with that which will control us in the purposes and ways of God. Rather than letting the things of the flesh and this world fill us we need to be filled with the Spirit so our actions will be under His control rather than the flesh. Thus, to be filled with the Spirit is to be controlled by the Spirit.

To "be filled with the Spirit" is a command to allow the Spirit to do His work. – Here is where this gets complicated. Both the negative and positive commands are present tense imperatives in the passive voice. In this context, present tense imperative verbs are those which are to be obeyed continuously or characteristically. The interesting part is that these commands are also in the passive voice. Passive voice verbs refer to something that is being done to the believer. Properly understood, this verse commands believer not to allow wine to fill them but rather to allow the Spirit to fill them. The verse could be paraphrased like this. *"Do not allow yourself to be characteristically controlled by the stuff of this world, but allow yourself to be characteristically controlled by the Holy Spirit."* So how do you obey such a command to be filled with the Spirit since it is something that only the Spirit can do in you? For us to obey this command we must put ourselves in a position whereby the Spirit can fill us. Perhaps this illustration will help you understand how this works.

During the COVID pandemic many people went to get vaccinated against this disease. I do not know of any who vaccinated themselves. No, those vaccinated drove to the vaccination site, filled out some forms, rolled up their sleeves, and allowed the nurse to inject the vaccine into their arms. Those who were vaccinated put themselves in the position whereby the nurse could vaccinate them. Similarly, to be filled with the Spirit believers must put themselves in a position whereby the Spirit can fill them. Believers must take the appropriate steps that will place them in the proper posture by which the Holy Spirit will do His work of filling them.

Steps believers must take to allow the Spirit to fill them. – Chafer presented three conditions essential for believers to be filled with the Spirit (Chafer, He That is Spiritual) (Chafer, Systematic Theology). These essential conditions are "Quench not the Spirit" (1 Thessalonians 5:19, KJV), "Grieve not the Holy Spirit" (Ephesians 4:30, KJV), and "Walk in the Spirit" (Galatians 5:16, KJV).

<u>"Grieve not the Spirit"</u> – The believer must seek to maintain a repentant heart towards sin. Paul wrote, "*And do not grieve the Holy Spirit of God, by whom you were sealed for the day of redemption*" (Ephesians 4:30, ESV). The context of this verse has to do with sin (Eph 4:25-32). Sin will grieve the Spirit of God. A believer that sins and shrugs it off without genuine confession and repentance grieves the Spirit of God. When the Holy Spirit is grieved, He will not fill the believer. In the case of guiding the believer in spiritual truth this creates a significant barrier.

The solution to this problem of grieving the Spirit is that of confession. John gave us this beautiful promise, "*If we confess our sins, he is faithful and just to forgive us our sins and to cleanse us from all unrighteousness.*" In the context of sin, confession, *homologeo*, is agreeing with God that your sinful actions are indeed wrong (Thayer p128). Yet confession without repentance is empty and powerless. Both confession and repentance are essential. They are to be vitally connected in the believer's life. Repentance, *metanoia*, refers to a change of mind (Thayer p117) that consequently results in a change in direction or action.

Those who harbor unconfessed and unrepentant sin cannot be filled with the Spirit since they are grieving the Spirit. Whether it be something big in one's eyes or small, sin will grieve the Spirit. I knew a preacher who once was doing a revival at a church. He stated that he went to the coke machine, put in a dollar, and two cans dropped out instead of one. Most people would have taken the two cans. However, this preacher was so concerned about taking something that was not his, which is stealing, that he took the extra can to the front desk. The person at the desk looked at him a little funny since no one ever came to the desk to return an extra can of soda. The point was that he did not want anything interfering with his being filled with the Spirit, which he rightly understood was essential for his ministry.

"Quench not the Spirit" – The believer must seek to receive biblical instruction and exhortation. See the full context of the phrase that Paul wrote to the believers in Thessalonica.

> "*Do not quench the Spirit. Do not despise prophecies, but test everything; hold fast what is good. Abstain from every form of evil*" (1 Thessalonians 5:19–22, ESV).

Here the use of the word "*prophecies*" is not to be confused with future telling. It has to do with "a gifted faculty of setting forth and enforcing revealed truth" (Thayer 161). Believers who summarily reject the clear instruction received from God's word will put out the Spirit's fire in their lives. This extinguishes the work of the Spirit in filling the believer.

I was a guest speaker in a church one time. As soon as I opened the Scriptures and began to preach a man in the back of the room waved his hand toward me in an expression of disgust and disapproval. This is a classic response of the heart that quenches the Spirit. This does not mean that believers should blindly do everything a teacher or preacher puts out. The Lord wants all believers to carefully examine everything they are taught. They are to "*hold fast*" to that which is good and reject that which is wrong. Remember that the Berean Jews were commended as more noble that those in Thessalonica because they listened to what Paul preached and examined it according to the Scriptures. They wanted to ensure that what Paul said was the truth (Acts 17:11).

In addition to hearing the word of God proclaimed, this implies that believers should be in the word of God themselves. They need to search for the truth of God's word beyond the weekly sermon alone. They must examine the biblical texts and apply them in life. Believers cannot stand on the crutch of ignorance.

Any believer who rejects the full teachings of the word of God is quenching the Spirit who empowers and illuminates truth. A believer cannot in his heart say, "I like everything I see in the Bible except this or that" or "I will not agree and adhere in that." To do so is to reject the infallible and inerrant word of God. How are believers to hear from the Lord if they reject the primary way the Lord reveals truth to them?

Those who do not accept the truth and authority of the word of God, the Bible, in its entirety need to repent of this sin. Those who do not pursue the truth of God's word with anticipation and passion must also repent. Here repentance has to do with changing one's attitude towards God's word. The result will be to accept that the Bible is absolute truth, that it is infallible, that it is unchanging, and that it is sufficient for us in every area of life. Moreover, this means that the believer will turn from a lethargic attitude towards God's word to one of seeking biblical truth with a revived zeal.

"Walk by the Spirit" – The believer must seek to avoid being controlled by the desires of the flesh. Paul wrote to the Galatians

regarding the struggles that all believers face between their own fleshly desires and that of the Spirit.

> *"But I say, walk by the Spirit, and you will not gratify the desires of the flesh. For the desires of the flesh are against the Spirit, and the desires of the Spirit are against the flesh"* (Galatians 5:16–17, ESV).

A believer who lives under the control of the flesh is living in opposition to the desires of the Spirit. Living in opposition to the desires of the Spirit will hinder the work of the Spirit in filling the believer. This will hinder the Spirit's work of illuminating the truth of God's word to the believer.

Here too the solution is confession and repentance. However, it is often difficult for the one who is controlled by the flesh to identify the problem. It is best to examine your life in view of motives. If the believer's motives are self-serving and not driven by the purposes of God there is a problem. If fleshly lusts are the driving factor of our lives, we are not able to be filled with the Spirit. Sometimes our emotions can be in control. When they are we will find ourselves out of control.

In the book of Galatians Paul lists the type of things that are manifested in the life of a person when the flesh is in control (Gal 5:19-21, 25). In Galatians 5:22-23 we see the fruit of the Spirit listed. Believers should prayerfully look through each of the things listed in Galatians 5:19-25 and conduct a spiritual inventory of their lives. When one identifies a failure, the proper remedy is to confess it to God and then seek His grace to reverse the tendency to fail in that area. In doing so the repentant one will then display the fruit of the Spirit.

There are certain believers that you will meet in life that just seem to exude godliness. Early in my Christian life I met such a man. He just seemed to have that certain presence about him. He spoke words of wisdom and demonstrated godliness. He outwardly demonstrated the humility and wisdom that only a man filled with the Spirit could. We can all be like that man. We can all be the spiritual person who is able to filter our thoughts so that our actions will display the fruit of righteousness.

Every one of us needs to live like the spiritual person that God has made us. To be that person one must be a true born-again believer and filled with the Spirit. To become a believer a person must trust in Jesus Christ alone for the hope of eternal life. To be filled with the Spirit there are three essential conditions. The believer must "Quench not the Spirit", "Grieve not the Spirit", and "Walk in the Spirit." It behooves all believers to do a prayerful self-examination to see if they have met these three conditions. When we have thoughts that require action, we must ask ourselves a question, "Am I living like a spiritual person?" We will greatly benefit from echoing the prayer of the Psalmist.

"Search me, O God, and know my heart! Try me and know my thoughts! And see if there be any grievous way in me, and lead me in the way everlasting!" (Psalm 139:23–24, ESV)

Filter number one is to answer the question, "Am I living like a spiritual person?" This is the most vital filter. However, this is just one. There are six more and each is important.

Filter #2 – Does the Bible say it is ok?

"For the word of God is living and active, sharper than any two-edged sword, piercing to the division of soul and of spirit, of joints and of marrow, and discerning the thoughts and intentions of the heart." (Hebrews 4:12, ESV)

One of my first fulltime jobs was as a retail sales clerk in a department store. I was assigned to the seasonal department, which sold toys, outdoor items, and etcetera. One of the things our department sold was bicycles. One day we received a new model of bicycle and the department manager asked another employee and me to assemble one for a store display. Well, we began putting it together intuitively, without instructions. When we got done, we had two parts left over. When we tried to pedal the bike, it was virtually impossible to use the pedals to make the rear wheel turn. It was then that we had a brilliant idea. "Let's look in the instruction booklet to see what these two parts are!" We discovered that they were the nylon-bearings for the rear wheel. We thought, "Well, it was just a display model anyway." So, we threw out the bearings and the packaging. Then we just put the bike up on the top display rack.

About a week later two women came into the store, saw that bike, and wanted to purchase one as a gift for a child. I told them that I would get one from the warehouse and bring it out to the register. However, they did not want one from the warehouse. They wanted the display model. I tried very hard to tell them that that bike was defective, that it would not work. Yet they would not listen. They left in a tizzy and came back a few minutes later with the store manager. He ordered me to give them the bike. I explained to the store manager that the bike had a problem but he would not listen either. He gave me a direct order to sell that display model to the two women. So, that is what I did.

I was not there when they brought back the defective bike. Yet this one thing I know. If we had just read the instructions before assembling the bike, we would have done it correctly and avoided the problem. It is the same way in the Christian life. The word of God gives us everything we need to know to negotiate our choices in life and keep us from failure. We just need to open the Bible, read it, and do what it says.

The Psalmist stated, *"Your word is a lamp to my feet and a light to my path."* (Psalm 119:105, ESV) The Bible will illuminate and guide us on the right path in life.

The previous filter, "Am I living like a spiritual person?" presented the primary one for examining our thoughts and ideas to determine if they align with what God wants us to do. The second filter is just as important as the first. Generally, one who satisfactorily passes through the first filter should naturally pass through this second one, which answers the question, **"Does the Bible say it is ok?"**

The Bible is one of the most vital filters used by spiritual people.

The writer of Hebrews directly wrote that the Bible is the primary and most effective tool for discerning the *"thoughts and intentions of the heart"* (Hebrews 4:12, ESV). The adjective the author of Hebrews used for, *"discerning,"* *kritikos*, comes from the noun *krites,* meaning a judge (Strong G2924) and refers to an ability to discern or judge (Thayer p106). The word of God, the Bible, is the God given filter for *"discerning the thoughts and intentions of the heart."* Thus, the second filter, "Does the Bible say it is ok?" is vital in decision making. Believers must use the Scriptures as a filter for their ideas, feelings, desires, and thoughts to ensure these align with God's purposes for us.

In using the Bible as a filter for our thoughts we must remember the vital importance of the first filter, "Am I living like a spiritual person?" This is because the Holy Spirit is the one who illuminates the truth of God's word to our hearts (John 14:26; 16:13; 1 Cor 2:6-16). If we do not pass through the first filter, we will not be able to trust our interpretation of the Scriptures in guiding our decisions.

Let me give you an example from the Bible regarding this. There was a man named Saul of Tarsus who after coming to faith in Jesus became an apostle. We know him as the Apostle Paul. Yet prior to his conversion Saul of Tarsus was a Pharisee, an expert in the Old Testament Scriptures. However, even though he was an expert in the Old Testament Scripture his interpretation and understanding of them was flawed. He followed the teaching of the Pharisees who viewed that legalistic obedience to the law would justify a person before God. Thus, he was a zealous persecutor of the church (1 Cor 15:9; Gal 1:13). He, as a Pharisee, was a religious person but not a spiritual person. After meeting the risen Lord on the road to Damascus Paul became a spiritual person through faith in the Lord Jesus Christ. He then had a complete turnaround in his understanding of the Old Testament Scriptures. He realized that Jesus was the Messiah and that it was faith and not works that saved a person. Understand this key point. Only the spiritual person through the illuminating work of the Holy Spirit can properly interpret the word of God.

I was in a church one time where the Pastor shared a story of a woman who called him because she had a dream. She believed that God spoke to her in the dream regarding something she was to do. It was good that she called her pastor for this is another filter that we will discuss later dealing with godly counsel. The pastor stated that he visited her and spent time searching the Scriptures to ensure that what she felt led to do was in agreement with God's word. The word of God is our essential filter.

Proverbs chapter two gives us some insight into this filter. Here we will learn how to get this filter and how to use it in practical terms.

Believers must attain the filter for use. (Proverbs 2:1-9)

This is a simple principle. You cannot use something that you do not have. We need to acquire the filter of the Bible. This requires two things. First, we must understand the sacred and majestic quality of the Bible. Second, we must passionately pursue it. Look at what the writer of Proverbs wrote in this regard.

> *"My son, if you receive my words and treasure up my commandments with you, making your ear attentive to wisdom and inclining your heart to understanding; yes, if you call out for insight and raise your voice for understanding, if you seek it like silver and search for it as for hidden treasures, then you will understand the fear of the Lord and find the knowledge of God."* (Proverbs 2:1–5, ESV)

Believers need a proper perspective of God's word. (Prov 2:1-5) – When we read Proverbs chapter 2, we see the majestic quality of the word of God. In these first five verses alone the writer of Proverbs speaks of it as having great value like *"silver"* and *"hidden treasure."* Those who search the word of God as *"hidden treasure"* will be in awe of God, and His infinite wisdom and knowledge.

Psalm 119 is the longest chapter of the Bible. It is filled with superlatives describing the majesty and sacredness of the word of God. Here are just a few of the many things the Psalmist noted. The Psalmist saw the word as having infinite value; *"The law of your mouth is better to me than thousands of gold and silver pieces"* (Psalm 119:72, ESV). He saw the righteousness of God in it, *"I know, O Lord, that your rules are righteous"* (Ps119:75). He saw it as eternal and established in the heavens, *"Forever, O Lord, your word is firmly fixed in the heavens"* (Ps 119:89, ESV), inferring that he saw every word of it as permanent, unchangeable, and absolute truth. He understood that the word would make him wiser than others who were without it, *"Your commandment makes me wiser than my enemies, for it is ever with me*" (Psalm 119:98, ESV). He understood that the word of God would satisfy the longings of the soul, "*How sweet are your words to my taste, sweeter than honey to my mouth!*" (Psalm 119:103, ESV).

The passage in Proverbs Chapter 2 indicates that the one who pursues knowledge, understanding, and wisdom will understand the fear of the Lord. Here, the fear of the Lord refers to respect and reverence for the Lord. When one has a deep desire for knowledge, he realizes that God is the only one who possesses such infinite and perfect knowledge. The Lord God is the omnipotent, omniscient, creator and sustainer of all things. Knowing this drives a person to seek the Lord for this knowledge. Moreover, the Lord has provided the possibility for us to gain this knowledge through the reading and study of His word, the Bible. He gives us the wisdom we need to negotiate every circumstance of life. He provides knowledge that gives us perception and discernment.

Many see the Bible as an old outdated book that is not relevant for the time in which we live. I thought the same until I read it. I discovered that the word of God contained deep truths for every area of life. People who view the Bible as outdated remind me of a story that I heard about an English traveler.

An English traveler was in a remote African village where the people formerly practiced cannibalism. As the traveler walked through the village, he observed a man who was a former cannibal sitting on a bench reading a book. The English traveler asked the man, "What are you reading?" The man said, "The Bible." The English traveler scoffed, shook his head, looked at the man, and stated, "Friend, that book has been long out of date in our country." The villager looked at the English traveler and replied, "Sir, if this book were out of date in this country you would have been someone's meal by now." Ok, think about it!

The Bible is not out of date. Its truths are timeless. It contains the absolute truth of God. It explains life. It contains the words of hope for eternal life. It has wisdom for every decision of life. The principles presented therein are still vital today. Paul wrote it.

"All Scripture is breathed out by God and profitable for teaching, for reproof, for correction, and for training in righteousness, that the man of God may be complete, equipped for every good work." (2 Timothy 3:16–17, ESV)

The word of God will make believers complete and it will equip them for the good works that God has prepared for them to do (Eph 2:10). People who make the statement that the Bible is out of date either have not read and studied it or have a predisposition against it as absolute truth.

One who is going to apply this second filter must have a proper perspective on the Bible. It is the absolute truth of God revealed to us. It is infallible, immutable, sufficient, and authoritative.

Believers need a passionate pursuit of God's word. (Prov 2:1-4, 9) – Unfortunately one thing seems to be missing in the lives of people, including those in the church. A 2014 Barna research study indicated that 79% of Americans believe the Bible is sacred and yet only 37% read it once a week or more. Of those who read it only 57% say they gave a lot of thought to how it might apply in life. (Barna Group 2014). Missing today is not an understanding of the majestic and sacred nature of the Scriptures. What is missing is a passion to hear from God through them. We live in a society that is becoming increasingly illiterate regarding the Bible.

In Proverbs 2:1-4, we see the phrase *"if you"* stated three times. These conditional phrases point to three things that the believers must have if they are to pursue the word of God with passion.

An inclined heart **(v1-2)** – One must have an openness to receive knowledge. *"if you receive my words and treasure up my commandments with you, making your ear attentive to wisdom and inclining your heart to understanding."* A person who will passionately pursue the truth of God's word must have open ears and an open heart. The word *"inclining,"* in the phrase *"inclining your heart,"* carries the idea of stretching out towards something. The implication is that this is a person who is reaching out for knowledge and is eager to grasp the teaching of God's word.

A humble spirit (v3) – A person must also have humility. The writer stated, *"if you call out for insight and raise your voice for understanding."* The only people who will call out for understanding are those who realize that they lack it. I cannot tell you how many times as a manufacturing manager that I saw people go off half-cocked with a little knowledge and totally mess things up in the factory. This happened because they would not humble themselves enough to ask questions and seek instruction. It is the same in trying to make decisions in life. Many people believe that they know the best way to run their lives and summarily reject the wisdom and knowledge contained in God's word. Not only must we be open to receive knowledge we must also understand how much we need the knowledge of God.

Diligent Effort (v4) – Pursuing the knowledge and wisdom of the Scriptures takes effort. It is not enough to be open to receiving knowledge and to know we desperately need it. We must also do something to get it. As it pertains to the knowledge of God, He has revealed this knowledge in His word, the Bible. We must do more than give a cursory glance to the Bible. We need to be on a passionate drive to grasp the truths contained therein. Are Christians today truly seeking for the deeper things of God in His word? I would say that on the average many believers have a lackluster drive for Bible reading and study.

I was in a meeting one time with about one-hundred Christian collegians. The leader of the ministry was giving away books and gifts to students who could respond correctly to certain questions. Those who raised their hands and gave the correct answer would receive a prize. I watched as the leader asked the group, "Who here has read the entire Bible through from cover to cover at least one time?" In the entire room only one student raised her hand. Not even the student leaders affirmed that statement. I surveyed leaders in a church one time and discovered that 80% of them had never read the Bible through even once.

In the pastorate I noticed that Christians would leave the Sunday service and sometimes forget to take their Bibles home. You know that only a small percentage ever collected the Bibles they left behind. After pastoring one church for ten years I had a stack of them in my office that were never claimed.

Believers need to get a passion for the word of God. When believers pursue the word of God with a passion, they will receive understanding and wisdom.

Blessings result from using the filter of God's word. (v5-22)

Once we have taken hold of this filter, we must use it or else it will not accomplish the task of filtering out the thoughts and ideas that we have. For believers who filter their thoughts and ideas through the word of God there are tremendous blessings. The writer of Proverbs describes these blessings.

"then you will understand the fear of the LORD *and find the knowledge of God... Then you will understand righteousness and justice and equity, every good path; for wisdom will come into your heart, and knowledge will be pleasant to your soul; discretion will watch over you, understanding will guard you,"* (Proverbs 2:5, 9–11, ESV)

God's word results in finding the knowledge of God (V5) – Who would not like to have the knowledge of God? Well, the truth is that the full extent of His knowledge is unattainable. That is because God's knowledge is infinite and we are not God. However, we can know much more than we do, a lot more. He has given us His word so that we can know everything necessary to negotiate life victoriously, fulfilling the purposes He has for us. When we read and study the Bible, we grow in this knowledge and can discern the thoughts and intentions of our hearts on any matter.

God's word gives understanding that keeps people on the right path (v9-10) – *"Then you will understand righteousness and justice and equity, every good path."* Here we see that understanding keeps a person on the correct path in life. The word translated as path refers to an entrenchment or a track (Strong H4570). It refers to a prepared way. The Lord has a correct prepared way for us to travel. It is the path of righteousness. He has endowed us with an intellectual and spiritual capacity to understand the way. Yet we cannot understand the way apart from the illuminating work of the Holy Spirit. When the Lord saves believers, He starts them on the correct path and His word provides the knowledge they need to stay on it. Along with this knowledge His indwelling Spirit gives every believer the inner strength needed to remain on this correct path.

God's word provides discretion that watches over us (v11a) – The writer of Proverbs wrote that *"discretion will watch over you."* The word of God gives believers that which is essential to exercise caution in life. It is this *"discretion"* that watches over believers' decisions, guarding them from wandering into unsafe territory. It will keep them within the boundaries of righteousness. The Scriptures establish boundaries for us to stay within as we journey in life. When we stay within these boundaries, we will discover that they keep us from unnecessary struggles and make our lives more joyful.

Studies have shown an interesting behavior of kids during school recess. Observers indicate that in playgrounds without a fence, children tend to huddle together in the center not playing out towards the perimeter. However, in playgrounds with a perimeter fence children will take full advantage of the entire area. The reason is that they have a better sense of security with a fence. Thus, they experience greater peace and joy because there are boundaries. The Scriptures set good boundaries for our safety that will give us peace, joy, and blessing.

God's word gives understanding that will guard us (11b) – The passage also tells us that *"understanding will guard you."* The word of God provides believers with understanding that will guard them while journeying through life. This works to keep believers from straying from the path of righteousness to the point of no return. Straying from the path of righteousness can be painful. When believers stray, they identify their wayward path confess and repent from it. Then they try very hard not to waver from the right path again.

However, some believers may stray from the righteous path and remain headed in a direction filled with pain and suffering. The Lord does not desire that any should experience the pain of travelling the unrighteous road. The word of God is a guard for believers to keep them from straying like a military sentry at a guard post, protecting them from the traps of the world.

While in military training at the Army Ranger School we spent some time practicing patrol techniques. On one of the exercises, we had a choice to take the trail on the ridge of the hills or go through the brush in the valleys. The trail on the top of the ridge was the longer route and the valley was the more direct route. Thus, the valley seemed like the quickest way to go, the expedient way. The patrol leader assigned for one exercise decided to take the direct route through the valley. However, the direct route was full of what we called "wait-a-minute-vines." Yes, they were thick briars. We were hung up in them beating our way through with much sweat and blood. By the time we got through the valley we were worn out and our arms were sliced up by the briars. It took twice as long to travel to the other ridge than if we had taken the high ground. It was not fun at all.

This is the way it is in life. We have various paths to take. Some are full of hazards and others are safe, full of blessing. God's word will guard us from needlessly choosing the wrong paths. This does not mean that we will never have difficulties. It does mean that the word of God will guard us from making decisions that will result in needless self-inflicted struggles.

Use the filter of God's word.

In a practical way, how do we use the filter, "Does the Bible say it is ok?" First, let us examine some things that we are not to do and then some things that we should do.

What not to do. – Have I ever told you how many failed things I have done? Most of these failures had to do with not seeking the Lord through Scripture and prayer. Here are some key things to avoid in seeking the truth of God from His word. Avoiding these will keep you from needless failure.

Do not act first and then seek the Scriptures. – This is one of our most common mistakes. It is when we have a thought, idea, or whim and proceed without seeking God and trying to determine what the Bible says about it. When we get an idea, we must pass it through the filter of the word of God. If it passes the question "Does the Bible say it is ok?" we can then proceed to the next filter.

While pastoring we began many new ministries. I confess now that we made some huge blunders in this. The largest one was beginning a ministry without significant time in searching the Scriptures and prayer. Most of the ministries started with this oversight were lack-luster and many failed. The ministries that prospered were the ones in which we spent considerable time in prayer. In this I am speaking of months of prayer and biblical deliberation, not hours. When we spent this much time seeking scriptural affirmation before starting something new, we saw much greater success.

Do not text proof. – To text proof means to take the preconceived thought, idea, or desire and set out to find a verse or passage that will approve it. We must always examine the Scriptures in context to determine the precepts that apply to the ideas we have. It is possible to prove anything we want by finding an isolated verse to prove our point.

The Seven Filters

I knew a man once who began an online relationship with a woman and decided to divorce his wife. He stood up in a church testimony time and stated this, "You shall know the truth and the truth shall set you free." He picked a verse, John 8:32, to justify divorcing his wife. This verse had nothing to do with permitting this man to divorce his wife so he could have a relationship with another woman. He was guilty of text-proofing.

Do not take passages out of context. – This is closely related to the previous issue. The point here is one of Bible interpretation. Remember this. Context is king. Every verse of Scripture must be interpreted with what comes before and after. It must also be interpreted in context with the totality of God's word, that is all sixty-six books of the Bible.

One of the passages that people often take out of context is Jesus' words given in the Sermon on the Mount. "*Judge not, that you be not judged*" (Matthew 7:1, ESV). In this passage Jesus intended for us to perform a serious examination of our own hearts to see the faults that lie there. Unfortunately, many engaged in sinful actions use this verse out of context to thwart off the attempts of others to confront them regarding their sin.

In the former example, where a man who used a verse to justify his divorce, he avoided other passages of Scripture that showed God's condemnation of divorce for willy-nilly reasons. If he had understood the context of John 8:32 and God's will regarding divorce as seen in many other passages he would have known that God hates divorce. He would have understood that his grounds for his action in no way lined up with the Bible.

What to do – Knowing what not to do is only part of the issue. Knowing what to do is essential. In short, the main thing to do with the word of God is to immerse yourself in it. If you wanted to dye a white garment red you would completely immerse the garment in red dye. You would not just dip one sleeve in the dye. In immersing the garment its appearance is transformed. Similarly, to truly experience the ability of the Scriptures to transform and provide guidance you need to dive in. You must become completely immersed in them.

Increase your overall knowledge of the Bible. – Some who are reading this book may not have studied the Bible from cover to cover. You must start somewhere. Get a good study Bible, one with cross-references, and perhaps a concordance in the back. Having one with wide margins to jot notes is useful. Begin by reading your Bible every day. Ok, if you miss a day don't worry. Just pick up where you left off. Underline the things that jump out at you in pencil. Jot notes in the margin.

Get involved in a Bible preaching and teaching church. If the pastor or teacher does not use the Bible, find another church. Get engaged in a small group study. In short, work at learning what the Bible says. You can take a course in how to study the Bible. Howard Hendricks has one called, "Living by The Book" (Hendricks). He also has a seven-session video and workbook for it. In it you will learn how to observe, interpret, and apply the truths of Scripture in life.

Make the Word of God part of your life. – Most often new believers will not have a real depth of biblical understanding. In the beginning you may want to pick up a book which will give you a topical index to the Scriptures. When you have a decision or question you can use it to look up a specific topic. Books like "Nave's Topical Bible" may be useful. With time and study, you will begin to grow in your understanding and knowledge of the Scriptures. Then you will need to rely less on these types of indices.

Ultimately, we should not have to use the Bible like a dictionary that sits on a shelf until we need to look up a word that we do not understand. We should progress to a point where the word of God becomes an integral part of our life. The Psalmist stated, "*I have stored up your word in my heart, that I might not sin against you*" (Psalm 119:11, ESV). Here, the Psalmist was so into God's word that it became his life. It was in his heart. He did not have to roll out the Scroll and search it. He already knew the precepts in it.

Therefore, we should be so entrenched in the word of God that it remains in us and will guard our hearts so we do the right things naturally. However, remember two things. First, every believer needs to continuously study God's word for we all, regardless of our level of maturity, are still growing in our knowledge of it. Second, we still need to prayerfully search the Scriptures when we are trying to discern the thoughts and ideas that we have. Yet our goal should be to grow to a point where the treasures of the Bible are stored in our hearts.

Prayerfully and scripturally examine every thought and desire. – We must carefully and prayerfully examine every thought or desire and bring it into submission with the will of God as revealed in His word, the Bible. Failure in this can be disastrous.

The word of God will help us understand the path that God wants us to take in life. We can stray from the righteous path and get caught up in the briar patch of sin. Sometimes the briar patch looks like the expedient way but it is a trap that will take us to a bad place. I have known many who have dabbled in worldliness only to find themselves trapped in an uncomfortable place. Some have joined in recreational substance abuse only to end up in full blown addiction. Some have tried sexuality in relationships only to find themselves with sexual disease or pregnancy. Some have married unbelievers only to struggle spiritually in their marriages. Some have gotten caught up in bitterness only to lash out in uncontrolled anger, landing them in jail. Seek the truth of God's word and stay on the right path.

Consider Saul, Israel's first king. Saul had everything going for him. However, he failed to filter his thoughts and ideas through God's word. We see this in the epitaph of his life.

> "*So Saul died for his breach of faith. He broke faith with the Lord in that he did not keep the command of the Lord, and also consulted a medium, seeking guidance. He did not seek guidance from the Lord. Therefore the Lord put him to death and turned the kingdom over to David the son of Jesse.*" (1 Chronicles 10:13-14, ESV)

Proverbs chapter two gives us some practical examples of how the Bible will protect us from making poor decisions. The writer tells us that it will deliver us *"from the way of evil"* (Prov 2:12a). The writer also tells us that we will be protected from the temptations of the world system (Prov 2:12b-15). He tells us that we will avoid being swayed by the ill-advised relationships that can take us off the path of blessing (Prov 2:16-19).

I had a man once who left his wife and moved in with the young woman next door. I called him on the phone to set up a meeting with him. He rejected the meeting. I then counselled him over the phone. His response was that God wanted him to be happy and that moving in with the girl next door made him happy. He claimed to find this truth from his understanding of God's word. May I say this? Nowhere in the Bible does it say that this man's actions were righteous. If the Bible says adultery is wrong, it is wrong! His actions were fleshly and foolish. They were in direct contradiction to the path of righteousness clearly presented in the word of God. Moreover, the wake of his decision left a path of pain and destruction.

As believers we must be like the wise person who built his house on the rock. That is the person who hears the word of the Lord and does what it says (Matthew 7:24-27). Use the filter of God's word and you will find blessing in life. When you have a thought or idea filter it through the Word of God before taking decisive action. D.L. Moody is recorded as saying, "The Bible will keep you from sin, or sin will keep you from the Bible." (Goodreads). Get into the Bible. It is the primary filter spiritual people will use to discern their thoughts and ideas to ensure they align with the will of God.

We have now looked at two filters for understanding whether these thoughts are from the Lord or not. When you have a thought or idea pass it through these filters before you proceed by asking two questions.

1. Am I living like a spiritual person?

2. Does the Bible say it is ok?

Answering these two questions correctly should filter out nearly all the incorrect thoughts or ideas. However, since we are all works in progress, growing in grace, we need to add some additional filters.

Steven B. Hankins, Th.D.

Filter #3 – Are my methods correct?

(Am I seeking and doing the right things the right way?)

"And when they came to the threshing floor of Chidon, Uzzah put out his hand to take hold of the ark, for the oxen stumbled. And the anger of the Lord was kindled against Uzzah, and he struck him down because he put out his hand to the ark, and he died there before God."
(1 Chronicles 13:9–10, ESV)

Sometimes all the good intentions in the world can still lead us to a disaster. Some years before surrendering to God's call to the pastorate I had a job as a plant manager in a factory that printed linerboard for corrugated boxes. Our printing press had cylinders upon which raised surface polymer printing plates were attached that would transfer the ink to the liner. The cylinders were driven by large gears which were designed to slide on the cylinder journals so the print position could be adjusted. One day, as I sat in my office doing paperwork, I heard something like large bells ringing in the plant. Being a bit puzzled I went to investigate.

I followed the bell sounds to the side of the machine where the crew was setting up a new print job. What I saw astounded me. There were two employees with sweat pouring off their brows swinging sledgehammers to drive the gears onto the journals. In the process they damaged the cylinder journals and gears. They had driven the gears onto the journals so tight that the machine controls could not move them while trying to make necessary adjustments. The crew and maintenance department labored for hours to get the gears back off the journals. The problem was that they did not follow the correct procedure to install the gears. They were to first inspect the journals and gears for damage, lubricate the journals, and then slide the gears on to the journals by hand. If they did not slide properly, they were to contact the maintenance personnel to correct the issue. To make a long story short, they were trying to do the right thing the wrong way.

This problem of trying to do the right thing the wrong way can be a major problem in life. Often people can have a noble goal and come up with an idea to accomplish it that is wrong. For instance, someone wants to get married. They know that marriage is a life-long commitment. So, the couple gets the idea, "Let's not get married right away. Instead let us live together for a year to see if we are fully compatible." I have talked to many couples with this flawed idea. The problem is that they had a noble goal but decided to pursue it in the wrong way. These types of ill-advised actions can lead to disaster.

In doing the right thing the right way there are two distinct but vitally connected issues. Believers must first know what the right thing to do is and then seek to do the right thing the right way.

Flawed Methods in Seeking the Voice of the Lord (1 Chronicles 10:13-14)

Sometimes people can seek to know the right things to do by using unbiblical methods. This is problematic. Trying to seek the voice of the Lord in a way contrary to biblical teaching will nearly always miss the mark. The Bible contains very specific examples of people who used incorrect methods to determine the will of God. We can learn much from these examples. First, we will look at some of these flawed methods. Then we will examine the correct biblical method for seeking the direction from the Lord.

Flawed Methods – Consider the epitaph of Saul, Israel's first king. In it we see a major flaw in his means of seeking direction.

> *"So Saul died for his breach of faith. He broke faith with the Lord in that he did not keep the command of the Lord, and also consulted a medium, seeking guidance. He did not seek guidance from the Lord.*

Therefore the Lord put him to death and turned the kingdom over to David the son of Jesse." (1 Chronicles 10:13–14, ESV)

The verse states that Saul consulted a medium and did not seek guidance from the Lord. This refers to a situation recorded in 1 Samuel 28. After the Lord had already rejected Saul as king and Samuel had died the Philistines were again threatening Israel and Saul was afraid. The Lord was not speaking to Saul. Therefore, he consulted a medium in Endor for guidance. He had the medium conjure up Samuel from the dead. The passage states that Samuel gave Saul a prophetic message that Israel would lose in battle and that Saul and his sons would die. What was the problem here? Saul felt that he needed guidance and the Lord was not speaking to him. So, Saul used a method to find direction that the word of God clearly prohibited.

The Problem of Divination – The Scriptures specifically forbid using divination to seek knowledge of the future and guidance (Leviticus 19:26, 31). It would be foolish to think that God would direct us through means that directly violates His word. We can never expect the blessings of God if we seek direction in such a forbidden way.

Many believers today are dabbling in things that they do not understand. What types of things are included in divination today? These are things like horoscopes, mediums, fortune tellers, tealeaf readings, tarot cards, Ouija boards, astrology, etc. Believers who are involved in these things must repent and cease these activities. Participation in these forms of divination is rebellion against the sovereign Lord. He has already given us everything we need to know in the Scriptures. Participation in divination is an entrance into a demonic realm that can trap people in something extremely evil.

What should Saul have done when he did not hear from the Lord? Well, the last thing he should have done was consult a medium. The problem with divination is that it demonstrates a lack of faith. Those who use divination show that they are not able to trust the sovereign will of the Lord for them. What should one do if they do not hear from the Lord? They should not move forward with something new until they do. They should continue to seek to hear from the Lord through prayer and the study of the Scriptures. They must learn to wait upon the Lord and to serve where they are until they do hear from Him.

I have had people come to me with some of the most bizarre ideas regarding hearing from the Lord. One person came into my office claiming to have heard from the Lord by random words coming into her head. She asked me what they meant. Frankly, they were such a mishmash of thoughts that it was impossible to run a thread through them. My suggestion was that she search the Scriptures and keep doing so until she saw something from the word of God that clarified things. I never heard back from her on this.

The Problem of Dependence on Signs – There is another issue that we need to understand. Some believers use signs in a very superstitious way. They do this under the guise of a fleece. You might remember that Gideon needed a sign to give him confidence in rallying Israel to contend with the Midianites. He asked for the sign of the fleece. Most of you know the story. If not, you can read about it in Judges 6. Here is the issue. There was no reason for Gideon to ask for this sign. This was because the Angel of the Lord had already communicated to him that he was going to successfully rally Israel and that they would win the battle. He should have listened to the Lord and responded by faith. The asking for a sign was a result of weakness in his faith. Yet here the Lord, in His mercy and grace, does work through a sign to affirm His plan.

Now there are some signs that we can use to affirm the will of the Lord. One may be providential circumstances that align with the purposes of God. For instance, if someone senses the Lord leading him to begin a Bible study that person should look to see if there are people interested in that type of study. Interested people would indicate that God is at work in it.

However, there are certain signs we use that are very sketchy. These are things like flipping coins. We cannot have true confidence in things like this. I heard of a man that was trying to determine what he was supposed to do by flipping a coin. When on the first flip he did not get the answer he desired, he said, "Ok, best out of three." The Lord wants us to understand His purposes and ways through the study of His word and then respond by faith.

On one occasion, someone told me that they saw a shape in the clouds of a unique figure. When I asked what the shape meant, she did not know for certain. Yet she made a guess that it was a sign of comfort. I have known others who made decisions based upon what they got from Chinese fortune cookies, the alignment of stars, etc. All these things are flawed methods that can lead people astray.

The problem of impatience. – This brings up Saul's major problem. His lack of faith resulted in an inability to wait on the Lord. Remember, this was his problem when he engaged the Philistines at Gilgal. He was to wait on Samuel to come and present the sacrifice but when he saw the Israelites fleeing, he became impatient. He could not wait and decided to present the sacrifice himself contrary to the word of God (1 Sam 13:8-15). Saul's lack of faith resulted in an inability to wait. Due to Saul's faithlessness as demonstrated in his improper action Samuel proclaimed the Lord's judgment on him.

> *"And Samuel said to Saul, 'You have done foolishly. You have not kept the command of the Lord your God, with which he commanded you. For then the Lord would have established your kingdom over Israel forever. But now your kingdom shall not continue. The Lord has sought out a man after his own heart, and the Lord has commanded him to be prince over his people, because you have not kept what the Lord commanded you.'"* (1 Samuel 13:13–14, ESV)

Saul lost the kingdom due to his lack of faith. God then planned to raise up a faithful man, one after God's own heart. His name was David.

The Seven Filters

There is a principle in this for us. We must learn to wait for the Lord. This is an issue of faith. If we are not hearing from the Lord there is a valid reason. In these cases, we are to seek Him patiently. The issue is one of trust. Even when He is silent, He is still at work in our lives. Thus, we must continue to seek the Lord and trust that He has things under control according to His sovereign program. The Lord will give strength to those who by faith can wait on Him. See His word as recorded by Isaiah.

"Even youths shall faint and be weary, and young men shall fall exhausted; but they who wait for the Lord shall renew their strength; they shall mount up with wings like eagles; they shall run and not be weary; they shall walk and not faint." (Isaiah 40:30–31, ESV)

Biblical Methods in Seeking the Will of God. – What are the methods we should use in seeking to hear from the Lord? We have spent much time on this in previous chapters of this book. However, we can learn much from seeing how George Muller sought to understand the will of God. Muller, a Christian evangelist in the early 1800's, was a man powerfully used by the Lord. It is stated that he cared for over 10,000 orphans in his lifetime, distributed nearly two-million Bibles and parts, supported missionaries, and established many schools that offered Christian education (Pierson p. 301). How did Muller seek God's will in doing this? He used the following steps, which outline key principles for believers.

1. I seek at the beginning to get my heart into such a state that it has no will of its own, in regard to a given matter. Nine-tenths of the trouble with people generally is just here. Nine-tenths of the difficulties are overcome when our hearts are ready to do the knowledge of what His will is.

2. Having done this, I do not leave the result to feeling or simple impression. If so, I make myself liable to great delusions.

3. I seek the will of the Spirit of God through, or in connection with, the Word of God. The Spirit and the Word

must be combined. If I look to the Spirit alone without the Word, I lay myself open to great delusions also. If the Holy Ghost guides us at all, He will do it according to the Scriptures and never contrary to them.

4. Next, I take into account providential circumstances. These often plainly indicate God's will in connection with His Word and Spirit.

5. I ask God in prayer to reveal His will to me aright.

6. Thus, (1) through prayer to God, (2) the study of the Word, and (3) reflection, I come to a deliberate judgment according to the best of my ability and knowledge, and if my mind is thus at peace, and continues so after two or three more petitions, I proceed accordingly.

(Muller , georgemuller.org/devotional/how-i-ascertain-the-will-of-God)

Here you see the purest biblical methodology described. You will note that Muller was patient. He did not proceed with anything until he had sufficiently sought the Lord. He did not rely on his own ideas and thoughts. Only those that aligned with the purposes of God as revealed in the word of God had merit. It all hinged on the word of God and the work of the Spirit of God. His methodology is a good pattern for every believer today. Apart from using a good biblical process like this we can stray far from the path that God has chosen for us. Every believer must endeavor to be led by the Spirit and be a serious student of the Bible.

Here is an example of how this worked in starting a new ministry in our church in New Hampshire. One of my deacons had a burden to begin a men's ministry. We had been meeting together every Friday morning to discuss God's word and to pray. When he informed me of his burden, we added this to our weekly prayer time. Yet this deacon went further and set up another Friday morning meeting with three other men from the church prior to our meeting. Every week they examined the Scriptures and prayed for direction regarding such a ministry. This deacon told me that he was not going to do anything until he sensed clear direction that was affirmed by the Bible. He prayed and sought the Lord's direction with these men for over a year. Then he came to me with what they believed the Lord would have them do. We launched the men's ministry soon afterward. It encompassed a men's Bible discussion group which was highly attended and a ministry to care for the needs of our widows. It was a great blessing to see what the Lord did through this ministry. Waiting, praying, and studying are all vital for gaining direction.

The Importance of Proper Methods in Doing the Will of God (1 Chronicles 13:1-14; 15:1-15)

Once believers have identified the right thing to do, they must proceed by doing the right things the right way. One of the critical errors that people make is this. Once they have a clear biblical understanding of what the Lord wants them to do, they often try to accomplish it in a way contrary to the will of God. They proceed through human expediency, neglecting the word of God. We see a prime example of this in David's attempt to bring the ark of God to Jerusalem.

> *"And David and all Israel went up to Baalah, that is, to Kiriath-jearim that belongs to Judah, to bring up from there the ark of God, which is called by the name of the Lord who sits enthroned above the cherubim. And they carried the ark of God on a new cart, from the house of Abinadab, and Uzzah and Ahio were driving the cart."* (1 Chronicles 13:6–7, ESV)

David, the king of Israel, was a man who sought to do the will of God. Having taken Jerusalem from the Jebusites he sought to make the city the capital and the religious center of the nation. Due to the ark's prominent place in the ordinances of worship he knew that they needed to have the ark of God in Jerusalem. However, the ark was not there. Under Saul the Philistines had captured the ark and later returned it to Israel. Yet during Saul's reign the nation neglected the ark's prominence in their worship. Understanding its importance, David properly sought to bring it to Jerusalem.

Similarly, as believers we are to seek the prominent things that God wants for us. We find these principles and practices in His word and we are to do them. This is no secret. There are thousands of precepts presented in the Scriptures. It is not possible to list them all. They include things like loving your neighbor, regularly meeting with other Christians, being good stewards of the resources God has given us, reaching people with the gospel, etc. However, often we try to accomplish these things in a way contrary to the Lord's plan. When this happens, the results can be disastrous. This is what happened in David's attempt to move the ark to Jerusalem. David made two attempts to move the ark to Jerusalem. The first one failed miserably. The second one succeeded.

Wrong methods and disastrous results. – In David's first attempt to move the ark to Jerusalem he gathered all Israel. He had them put the ark on a new oxcart. What could be better than using a brand new and unused oxcart to move the ark of God? They proceeded with rejoicing, singing, and the playing of music. It was a grand and glorious picture, was it not? We might think that everything was perfect. Yet it was not.

> "*And when they came to the threshing floor of Chidon, Uzzah put out his hand to take hold of the ark, for the oxen stumbled. And the anger of the Lord was kindled against Uzzah, and he struck him down because he put out his hand to the ark, and he died there before God.*" (1 Chronicles 13:9–10, ESV)

When the procession reached the threshing floor of Chidon, Uzzah, one of the men driving the cart, reached out his hand to steady the ark because the oxen stumbled. When he did this the Lord struck him dead. As a result, they stopped the procession and left the ark in the household of Obed-Edom for three months.

What was the problem? Why did the Lord do this? It had to do with the holiness of the ark and God's prescribed method for

The Seven Filters

moving the ark. David tried to move the ark to Jerusalem, which was the right thing to do, but he chose to do it in the wrong way. The Law given to Moses from God explained the exact way Israel was to transport the ark. Only the Levites were to transport the ark of God and for this they were to carry it using poles supported on their shoulders. David chose to do the right thing but they did it in the wrong way by placing the ark on the oxcart.

Consider the human wisdom in this attempt to bring the ark to Jerusalem. Would it not be much easier to transport the ark on a cart than by carrying it with poles on the shoulders of the Levites? Moreover, it was a brand-new cart. Yet this was not the prescribed way the Lord wanted the ark to be moved. The results were disastrous. Uzzah died and there was a three-month delay in accomplishing the good thing David wanted to do. This is the problem with human expediency and ignorance of the right methods. When we try to do the right things in the wrong way, we generally find failures, difficulties, and delays in getting the right things accomplished.

I have personally experienced this in the area of resolving conflict between people. Too many times I have fallen into the trap of being the "monkey in the middle." Two people have a problem. One would come to me and say, "You must straighten this out. Joe has done something wrong. Go to him and fix it." So, I would go to Joe and present the problem. Then Joe would respond, "You do not know the full story. He started it." So, I would go back to the initial complainer who just pointed the finger at Joe. I would end up wasting countless hours bouncing back and forth between two people who had a problem with one another. Do you see the issue? I got caught up in trying to resolve a problem between two people in a way contrary to the method Jesus prescribed. You can see it in Matthew 18:15-17. By trying to resolve the conflict as an intermediary rather than making the people sit down and resolve their differences, as the Bible clearly tells us, the problem was not being resolved. It just caused the problems to fester and consequently delayed resolution in the conflict.

On another occasion, as the director of the single adult ministry at a church, I sat with a small group of our singles and discussed ministry plans. One of the things we talked about was how to grow the singles ministry. There were still many who were not participating. One of our more vocal group members shouted out, "We have to lure them in like the devil." Well, we did not pursue that thought but I did wonder what he meant. Was it dancing girls, a kegger, or something else? It does sound ludicrous but have we not seen churches doing things contrary to Scripture to grow attendance? I know of a growing church where the pastor stated, "I do not preach on bad things." This was his explanation for their growth. Yet does not the Bible tell us to preach the full counsel of God?

Therefore, we must do the right things the right way. What we attempt to do with human expediency usually is to take the easy way or a shortcut. However, any variance from the ways of God will end up taking us off the correct path and lead to delays, difficulties, and failures.

Right methods and blessed results. – In 1 Chronicles 15 we see that David realized that three months earlier they used the wrong method to transport the ark. Thus, he planned to move the ark again. Only this time things would be different.

> *"Then David said that no one but the Levites may carry the ark of God, for the Lord had chosen them to carry the ark of the Lord and to minister to him forever. And David assembled all Israel at Jerusalem to bring up the ark of the Lord to its place, which he had prepared for it."*
> (1 Chronicles 15:2–3, ESV)

David demanded that they move the ark in accordance with the methods prescribed by God. The Levites consecrated themselves. They carried the ark with poles as prescribed in the Law. This time, the movement of the ark had a much different tone.

> *"So David and the elders of Israel and the commanders of thousands went to bring up the ark of the covenant of the* LORD *from the house of*

The Seven Filters

Obed-edom with rejoicing. And because God helped the Levites who were carrying the ark of the covenant of the LORD, *they sacrificed seven bulls and seven rams. . . . So all Israel brought up the ark of the covenant of the* LORD *with shouting, to the sound of the horn, trumpets, and cymbals, and made loud music on harps and lyres.*" (1 Chronicles 15:25–28, ESV) (1 Chronicles 15:25–26, 28-29 ESV)

Now they rejoiced as they completed the journey to Jerusalem and returned the ark to its preeminent place in the ordinances of worship.

Years ago, I worked for a company headquartered in Zurich Switzerland that sold industrial printing presses. In this work I often had to escort various suppliers to the factory. I remember having to go to the airport in Minneapolis Minnesota to pick up one of the supplier's representatives. On the drive from the airport, I mentioned my involvement in the church as a believer in Jesus. He proceeded to tell me all about his being a Baptist. We had a nice discussion. After meeting the people in the factory, the plant manager suggested that we all go out to lunch together. This we did.

At lunch the people from the factory began telling obscene jokes and stories. I kind of knew this was going to happen. So, I sat there just neutral and not affirming them. I expected the supplier's representative to do the same and hopefully quiet the rhetoric by his silence. Unfortunately, this is not what happened. He laughed at their crude jokes and even told some of his own. I guess he thought this was good salesmanship. I was shocked. Yes, it was good for him to want to make the sale of his products but it was not good to do so with corrupting talk (Eph 4:29), which compromised his testimony. I do not think he ever made one sale to this prospective customer. Trying to do the right things the wrong way, that is the way contrary to righteousness, always misses the mark.

Compromise in methods happens all the time but it should not. The Scripture states, "*There is a way that seems right to a man, but its end is the way to death"* (Proverbs 14:12, ESV). Compromising righteousness will fail. God's ways are not our ways. They are infinitely higher than ours are.

> *"For my thoughts are not your thoughts, neither are your ways my ways, declares the Lord. For as the heavens are higher than the earth, so are my ways higher than your ways and my thoughts than your thoughts."* (Isaiah 55:8–9, ESV)

Our job is not to use human wisdom to fulfill the right things that God calls us to do. Our job is to do the right things the right way and trust God for the results. God's ways may not always seem the most expedient or even the best ways to accomplish things. This is because His ways conflict with the ways of this world system.

Consider Paul's words to the Romans regarding dealing with an enemy.

> *"Beloved, never avenge yourselves, but leave it to the wrath of God, for it is written, 'Vengeance is mine, I will repay, says the Lord.' To the contrary, 'if your enemy is hungry, feed him; if he is thirsty, give him something to drink; for by so doing you will heap burning coals on his head."* (Romans 12:19–20, ESV)

From the standpoint of human reasoning, the system of this world, caring for an enemy does not make any sense at all. Yet it is what God tells us to do. We are to do the right things God's way and trust Him for the results. In theological terms that means we are to be driven deontologically (by duty) not teleologically (by end results). The end results do not justify the means. We are to do things God's way and trust Him with the results.

Filter #1 – Am I living like a spiritual person?

Filter # 2 – Does God's word say it is ok?

Filter #3 – Are my methods correct?

(Am I seeking and doing the right things the right way?)

Filter #4 – Does it take true faith?

"So we are always of good courage. We know that while we are at home in the body we are away from the Lord, for we walk by faith, not by sight."
(2 Corinthians 5:6–7, ESV)

In the Movie "Indiana Jones - The Last Crusade," Indiana Jones came to a crisis point in his quest for the holy grail. His father was seriously wounded and would die apart from a miracle. The only hope was that Indiana could get to the cavern in which the holy grail, the cup that Christ used at the Last Supper, was located, and bring it back filled with water. The thought was that by drinking from that cup his dad's wounds would be healed.

There was only one problem. To get to the cavern Indiana had to run through a series of hazards. To avoid these, he had a series of mysterious clues. He negotiated all of them and then came to a great crevasse with no apparent way to cross. He saw the entrance to the cavern straight ahead. As he looked down, he saw that to step forward meant certain death. Yet the clue he had at that point was that he must take a leap of faith.

Indiana is faced with no option. He either steps out by faith or his father dies. So, he stepped out into the crevasse. Then he discovered an unseen bridge across the crevasse, one that was carefully camouflaged into it. Then he successfully negotiated the crevasse into the cavern.

This scene in the movie gives us a unique illustration of what faith is about. The writer of Hebrews gives us this insight into the meaning and the walk of true faith.

"Now faith is the assurance of things hoped for, the conviction of things not seen . . . And without faith it is impossible to please him, for whoever

would draw near to God must believe that he exists and that he rewards those who seek him." (Hebrews 11:1, 6, ESV)

Discerning the thoughts and ideas we have requires true faith. The question is, "What is true faith?" While we can define true faith, unfortunately there are many impostors of true faith that abound in Christian circles. Let us first look at what true faith is, how we are to live by it, and then understand the impostors that we must carefully avoid.

Understanding True Faith

The writer of Hebrews gives us this definition of faith. *"Now faith is the assurance of things hoped for, the conviction of things not seen"* (Hebrews 11:1, ESV). The Greek word translated faith, *pistis*, refers to a firm persuasion or conviction (Thayer p147). This definition highlights two key characteristics of true faith.

True faith is a confidence. – The writer tells us that *"faith is the assurance of things hoped for."* The word assurance, *hupostasis*, refers to a substructure, a support or foundation (Strong G5287). Faith is the foundation for our hope. Hope in the Christian life is not like the "I hope so" used by the unbelieving. In the Christian context hope is that for which we wait with joy and confidence. Therefore, true faith is the confident foundation for the things God has promised. Faith is a gift of God given to us who believe so we can have confidence in His promises. One huge problem for people is that of ignorance. Many do not know the Bible and the thousands of promises that are contained in it. Depending upon the source, some have numbered the promises of God at 7,000 or more. If believers truly understood the magnitude of God's promises their Christian walk would be much different.

True faith is a conviction. – The writer goes on to say *"the conviction of things not seen."* Conviction, *elegchos*, refers to a proof or evidence by which a thing is tested (Strong G1650). Here the words, *"not seen"* literally mean the things that we cannot see with our eyes. In a metaphoric sense the phrase means not seen with the mind's eye or unable to understand mentally. Faith is that gift of

God by which we have the proof of things that the natural man cannot understand. This is vital for us to understand because the ways of God are infinitely higher than our ways. Therefore, based upon our finite view of the circumstances and situations around us, we cannot always fathom what God is doing in the big picture. This is because His ways are infinitely higher than our ways are (Isaiah 55:8-9).

In a way this is like the 1000-piece jigsaw puzzle. If you did not have the picture of the finished assembled puzzle and you picked up one piece of the puzzle at random you would have no idea what the big picture was. God is sovereign over the big picture and it is beautiful. We are just called to manage our piece of the puzzle. We do this by faith, believing that the result is just as beautiful as God has told us in His word. Here faith is the answer. Faith confidently affirms the purposes and ways of God even when we cannot understand them in the big picture.

Principles for Using the Faith Filter

The writer of Hebrews also gave us some key principles necessary for using the faith filter.

"And without faith it is impossible to please him, for whoever would draw near to God must believe that he exists and that he rewards those who seek him" (Hebrews 11:6, ESV).

Using the faith filter requires devotion. – There is a direct link between our ability to walk by faith and our personal devotion to the Lord. The writer stated, *"without faith it is impossible to please him, for whoever would draw near to God must believe he exists."* The author indicates that faith is required to please God and this involves drawing near to Him. In Hebrews Chapter 5 the author gave the example of Enoch. Enoch pleased God. What was it about Enoch's life that pleased Him? We see this in Genesis 5:24, *"Enoch walked with God, and he was not, for God took him."* Enoch walked with God. This is a picture of complete and continuous devotion to God that results in intimate continuous communion with God.

My wife and I have the blessing of living in an area where we can walk to the ocean. We try, weather permitting, to go nearly every day for an hour stroll along some stretch of the Atlantic Ocean. One of the interesting things about going for a walk with someone is that you are in close contact with each other. Consequently, it is one of the best places for communicating with each other. Enoch walked with the Lord. His connection with the Lord was continuous and intimate. This undoubtedly opened a clear channel of communication with the Lord. This is what we are to pursue in our walk of faith. When we are devoted to God as Enoch was and walk with God as Enoch did, we will trust Him in every area and circumstance of life. We will trust in His sovereign oversight and plans. Moreover, in this walk we have a special intimate connection and channel of communication by which we can hear from Him.

Using the faith filter requires standing on God's promises. – The writer goes on to say that one must "*believe*" God "*exists and that he rewards those who seek him.*" It is not possible to have faith in anything that you do not believe exists. We must believe that God exists as the true God who is omnipotent, omniscient, omnipresent, immutable, infinitely holy, good, true, merciful, and just. A proper comprehension of the awesome wonder and magnificence of God is essential in a believer's faith walk.

Moreover, the author tells us that God rewards those who seek Him. Here again are two interesting words. "*Rewards*," *misthapodotes*, refers to one who remunerates, that is one who pays equivalent for services rendered (Strong G3406). God is the faithful Master who, by His grace, rewards those who seek Him.

The verb "*seek*," *ekzeteo*, is a stronger word than what generally comes to mind. It carries the idea of seeking after or searching with diligence (Strong G1567). One time, I lost my car keys and needed to drive to a meeting. I was in a bit of a panic. So, what did I do? Well, I did not sit back on our sofa with my legs propped up on the coffee table, watching television. No, I diligently searched all over the house looking for the keys with a great sense of urgency. This is the type of passion that must be in the lives of believers in seeking God. It is those who seek Him with passion that will experience great reward.

Believers who will effectively use the faith filter are those who have a heart of devotion for God. They will have a passion for the things of God and will pursue God with the same passion. These are the type of people who will be able to use the faith filter to sort out their thoughts and ideas to ensure they conform to the will of God.

Proper Perspectives in Using the Faith Filters – Characteristics of True Faith

Sometimes believers can get off track when using the faith filter because they lack a proper perspective of faith. We can understand this in two ways, from the positive and from the negative. From the positive we see true perspectives on faith. From the negative we see the impostors that we must avoid. Let us first look at the positives.

True faith is a characteristic walk not an occasional one. – I used to think that faith was something that we used only at certain times. This included times when we had a crisis and needed a miracle. It was something to use when we needed God to do the impossible. However, the word of God teaches us that faith is to be operative 24/7. The Scriptures say, *"we walk by faith, not by sight."* The present tense use of the verb *"walk"* implies a continuous and characteristic activity. The verse does not tell us to *"walk by faith"* occasionally or only when needed. Perhaps the verse is better translated as *"we characteristically walk by faith."*

This faith walk involves our thought life, our conversations, our work habits, our courteous witness in our travels, etc. It involves the conscious recognition that the Lord God is sovereign over all our affairs. It involves the knowledge that He is present with His children always and that He is at work in every situation in every moment of the believer's life. It is that understanding that God does have our best interest in mind and continuously works in every situation for our benefit (Rom 8:28) whether we understand it or not.

Moreover, the faith walk involves the believer's continual trust in the ways of God as revealed in His word. It involves the pursuit of understanding His ways with a deep desire to live according to them. It is a humble perspective regarding one's own weaknesses, realizing that only by trusting the Lord will the believer be able to live victoriously regardless of life's struggles. It also is a humble perspective in realizing that we are spiritually frail and even though we try hard not to sin we still will on occasion fail. Yet even in our failures we recognize the beauty of God's amazing grace to lift us up and put us back on solid ground. Faith is a characteristic walk that encompasses the totality of the true believer's life.

Faith always requires waiting on God. – While the walk of faith is to be a 24/7 thing, there are some special bold demonstrations of this in our daily walk. One of these is waiting on the Lord. Perhaps the greatest expression of faith is to patiently wait on the Lord for something, especially when the time of waiting is excruciating.

Shortly after the Lord saved me in 1983 the pastor of our church gave me an opportunity to be certified as a Teacher/Trainer of Evangelism Explosion (EE). Ultimately, I headed up the EE equipping ministry in the church. One of the things I did for this was give the assignments to the visitation teams. For this I kept a stack of contact and referral cards for people we might visit on Thursday evenings.

One week I received a referral card that did not give me much hope for a successful visit. In fact, I kept putting it at the bottom of the stack of the referral cards. Yet all week long that card kept ending up at the top of the stack. I really do not know how. So, that Thursday evening I gave that referral card to our pastor and his team. They went out after prayer to visit the person referred on that card. Later that evening they came back to report on their visit rejoicing as the man on that card received Christ during their visit.

The Seven Filters

They shared that after he believed he immediately called his father-in-law in Seattle Washington. He explained that his father-in-law had been praying for his salvation faithfully for 60-years. Wow, 60-years of faithful prayer. I wonder how many of us would have given up after praying for a person's salvation after a year, or even months or weeks.

Unfortunately, we tend to grow weary in waiting. Yet true faith has an ability to wait on God for results even when it seems like our efforts are futile. This issue of waiting on God is huge. It is difficult to stand firm, continuing to hope and obey when the circumstances prompt us to quit. Faith presses the believer to work through the times of waiting because we understand that God is sovereign over them.

Faith requires that we trust God and not ourselves. – This is perhaps the most difficult distinction of true faith. I have met people who think that if they just pray hard enough or believe hard enough that they can make God do what they think is right. This is far from the way faith works. God is not obligated to do what we want. He alone is sovereign over the affairs of men. Look at what the Psalmist stated.

> *"My frame was not hidden from you, when I was being made in secret, intricately woven in the depths of the earth. Your eyes saw my unformed substance; in your book were written, every one of them, the days that were formed for me, when as yet there was none of them."* (Psalm 139:15–16, ESV)

Honestly, it is difficult to comprehend how this works. How the Master has a sovereign plan and how that perfectly fits the decisions men make one cannot adequately explain. However, this one thing we know. The faith walk is not about bending God's will to our will. It is about conforming our will to His. In other words, we must trust Him in everything and seek to join Him in His sovereign program.

Moreover, it is not the greatness of our faith, as we understand it, that moves mountains. Look at the incident with

Jesus' disciples trying to deliver a demon from a man's son. Jesus was coming down from the Mount of Transfiguration with John, Peter, and James. Down in the valley He saw the other disciples in conversation with a man. Jesus asked the man what they were discussing. The man responded that he brought his son to the disciples but they failed in delivering the boy from an oppressing spirit. Jesus then rebuked the spirit and the boy was healed instantly (Matt 17:14-19). Following this the disciples were perplexed and ask Jesus, *"Why could we not cast it out?"* (Matthew 17:20, ESV). See how Jesus answered their question.

> *"He said to them, 'Because of your little faith. For truly, I say to you, if you have faith like a grain of mustard seed, you will say to this mountain, 'Move from here to there,' and it will move, and nothing will be impossible for you.'"* (Matthew 17:20, ESV)

His answer seems a bit strange when you consider what He told them. He stated that it was because of their little faith and then He told them that they only needed *"faith like a grain of mustard seed"* to move mountains. A mustard seed is the smallest of seeds, only 1 to 2 millimeters in diameter. Jesus did not tell them they needed faith like a large seed, such as a date or palm seed. He did not use a large metaphor such as they needed faith the size of a house or palace. No, He spoke of having faith like the smallest of seeds. Why? It was because the size of their faith was not the issue. What was the issue?

To understand this, we must answer two questions. The first is, "Who it is that moves mountains?" The second is, "Who it is that decides whether a mountain is to be moved in the first place?" The answer to both questions is the same. The Lord our God is the one who moves mountains and He is also the one who decides when and what mountain is to be moved. In other words, the power of faith to move mountains did not lie in the disciples. The faith to move mountains is not faith in oneself. It is not faith in one's faith. It is faith in the One who has the power to move the mountains, the Lord our God. He moves in accordance with His sovereign will in His own perfect way according to His own precise timing.

We do not know what specifically was wrong with the disciples' faith in that incident. They may have been trusting in their own abilities, some spoken formula, or their previous successes. Perhaps they just gave up when they did not see an instantaneous deliverance. The only thing that we can conclude is that faith that moves mountains is faith in the Lord our God and not in ourselves.

D.A. Carson illustrated this issue of true faith in speaking of a picture of two Jews at the time of the first Passover. They were discussing the decree for the people to put blood on the door posts and lintels of their homes so the angel of death would pass over them. Both men had firstborn sons. One was nervous about what was going to happen that night and the other was positive that the angel of death would pass over his home. Both the nervous man and the confident man put the blood of the lamb on the door posts and lintels of their homes. Carson then asked the question, "Which one lost his son?" The answer was "Neither." The point of the story is this. It is not the intensity of one's faith but the object of one's faith that saves. (Taylor and Carson) (Carson). You can view the entire thought on YouTube. True faith is that which trusts the Lord our God and not ourselves.

Improper Perspectives in Using the Faith Filter. – The Impostors of Faith to Avoid

Like anything there are some impostors to true faith. Having dealt with the essence of true faith, now we must look at some examples of faith impostors. These are things that sneak into Christendom very subtly and confuse many. The Bible gives us some glaring examples of this in the Israelites efforts to enter the Promised Land on their first attempt. Here, Israel's faithlessness exposes two very distinct faith impostors.

Impostor #1 is walking by sight and not by faith. – One of the greatest impostors of true faith is to walk by sight. This means to have faith in the things we can see and understand from a human perspective. When we walk by sight, we are having faith in ourselves to do the things that we feel are humanly possible. In this case human reasoning corrupts true faith. We see this as the nation of Israel approached the Promised Land, Canaan.

Let us remember that true faith confidently affirms the purposes and ways of God even when we cannot understand them in the big picture. The two key parts of this are confidence in the promises of God and conviction of the things not fully understood.

When the Lord led Israel to the Promised Land, He ordered Moses to send out spies into the land. I always wondered why the Lord sent the spies into the land. Why not just tell the nation to enter and take the land? After all, the Lord was going to give them the land by His mighty power in driving out the inhabitants before them. I can only suggest a couple of reasons. It might have been a testing of the nation's faith so that they would understand the nature of their own hearts. It also might have been so they would see the enormity of the task and enter by faith so God would get the glory alone.

Well, Moses sent out the 12 spies. They spent 40 days scoping out the land and upon returning gave a report to the nation. They reported that the land was fruitful and prosperous. However, ten of the spies gave a doom and gloom report. They said the cities were fortified and that there were fierce people in the land, which included a race of giants. They said that it would be suicide to attempt such a conquest. On the other hand, Caleb stated that they should go immediately and take possession of the land for God would give it to them.

Yet the nation did not listen. They panicked, became fearful and sorrowful, they grumbled, and initiated a rebellion against Moses, which ultimately was a rebellion against the Lord. They appointed another leader and determined to go back to Egypt. Both Joshua and Caleb pleaded with the nation not to rebel against the Lord but to trust the Him and enter the land. Rejecting Joshua

The Seven Filters

and Caleb's plea the nation proceeded with their rebellion. As a result, the Lord pronounced a judgment on the nation. The people would not enter the Promised Land. They would wander in the wilderness for 40 years until every person 20 years of age and older died, except for Joshua and Caleb.

The problem was that the rebellious nation was walking by sight and not by faith. God had promised the nation that He would drive out the inhabitants before them until they possessed the land (Ex 23:27-31). See the Lord's words of promise as recorded in the book of Exodus.

> *"And I will send hornets before you, which shall drive out the Hivites, the Canaanites, and the Hittites from before you. I will not drive them out from before you in one year, lest the land become desolate and the wild beasts multiply against you. Little by little I will drive them out from before you, until you have increased and possess the land."* (Exodus 23:28–30, ESV)

The Israelites had the direct promise of God. Their problem was that they allowed what they saw in the land to put a cloud over their hearts so they would not trust the Lord according to His promise. This is sort of amazing when you consider what they saw the Lord do in delivering them from the Egyptians. He continuously demonstrated His awesome and miraculous power to them throughout their journey to the Promised Land. However, here they failed to trust Him.

This is not unusual for people, even believers. We tend to do everything based on what we see. Here is an example. The Scriptures teach us to do everything possible to be at peace with others in our relationships. We are to win over evil with good (Rom 12:14-21). However, when push comes to shove, we tend to hold grudges, avoid people, and sometimes retaliate. We often do this even though the Scriptures indicate that the best way, the higher way, is to do the opposite.

Often the Lord will grant churches a vision for reaching their communities. Yet people will say things like, "We've never done it that way before," rather than examining the Scriptures and praying for insight. I was in a church that had an abundance of money in the bank. There were a lot of children in the community. There was also a man in that church who the Lord was using mightily to reach these children. There was a proposal to take some of the savings and build a bubble-gym on the property to better engage the children and families of the community. The board of the church shot down the idea stating that they needed the money in the bank as a safety net just in case giving went down. To paraphrase it in different terms, "We need to keep all our money in the bank just in case the Lord does not provide." Yet the Lord promises to provide everything needed for those who partner with Him in ministry (2 Cor 9:8; Phil 4:19). The church shut down a short time later and turned everything over to another church in the area. Their problem? They did not trust God at His word.

Impostor #2 is presumption and not true faith. – There is a second devastating impostor to true faith. It is presumption. We also see this in the biblical record of the Israelites failure to enter the Promised Land. After rebelling against the Lord, Moses relayed the judgment of the Lord on them for their faithlessness. Remember the judgment was that the rebellious ones who were 20-years of age and older, except for Joshua and Caleb, would wander in the wilderness for 40-years until the faithless generation perished. None of them would enter the Promised Land.

Now the people were not very happy about the thought of wandering in the wilderness. So, after hearing the judgment of the Lord from Moses they mourned greatly. When they rose early in the morning, they had a change in mind. They said, *"Here we are. We will go up to the place that the Lord has promised, for we have sinned"* (Numbers 14:40, ESV). The only problem was that the Lord had already pronounced the judgement for their rebellion. Moses explained that the Lord's judgment was final and that by going they were transgressing the command of the Lord. Moses warned them that they would be struck down if they went ahead with this plan because the Lord would not be with them.

The Seven Filters

Yet the people did not listen to Moses' warning and decided to go anyway. Scripture indicates the huge flaw in their decision.

"But they <u>presumed</u> to go up to the heights of the hill country, although neither the ark of the covenant of the Lord nor Moses departed out of the camp" (Numbers 14:44, ESV).

The key word here is *"presumed."* They *"presumed"* to go and that the Lord would give them the victory. Presumption is an impostor for true faith. The result of their presumption is written.

"Then the Amalekites and the Canaanites who lived in that hill country came down and defeated them and pursued them, even to Hormah" (Numbers 14:45, ESV).

This is the problem of presumption. Presumption occurs when we decide to do something and expect God to join us with His blessing. True faith is seeing where God is at work and then joining Him there. Presumption is seeing where we want to go and then expecting God to join us. Presumption is sure to fail for presumption is not true faith.

One night I witnessed an example of presumption while watching television. A television preacher quoted a verse of Scripture and said something that astounded me. He quoted Proverbs, *"A man's heart plans his way, But the Lord directs his steps"* (Proverbs 16:9, NKJV). Following the reading of this verse he went on to say, "This means that if you have a plan, God will bless you." Then he proceeded to give a 40-minute message on how to make a strategic plan to do something. He indicated that if people made a proper plan, they would experience the blessings of God.

The problem with this message is that it overlooked the sovereignty of God. There is nothing wrong with planning. In fact, it can be a good thing. However, man's planning does not guarantee the blessings of God. He is not obligated to bless manmade plans. This statement and the subsequent message by the TV preacher are examples of a flaw that many people have regarding faith. It is one of presumption.

We as believers can so easily fall into this terrible trap of presumption. It happens when church people come up with a ministry idea or follow another church's ministry model and believe that by doing so the Lord will bless it. It happens when people decide to purchase a lottery ticket and believe if they pray hard enough that God will make their number win. Presumption boils down to the same problem as all faith failures. It is a trust in oneself. True faith is trusting in God's sovereign plan, in seeking and doing His will, and in trusting Him regardless of the way things may look.

Let us look at how all parties applied the filters. First, the ten spies and the nation did not apply them. If they had applied them, they would have filtered out the fears of their perceived impossible circumstances. They would have filtered out their pessimism. They would have understood the power of God and that He would fulfill His promise to drive out the inhabitants before the nation. Last, having understood the judgment of God for their faithlessness, they would have filtered out presumption and submitted to the judgment God pronounced upon them.

The good news is that two men, Joshua, and Caleb, applied the faith filters successfully. Theirs would be a delay in entering the Promised Land because of the faithlessness of the nation. However, because of true faith they would enter the Promised Land 40 years later. Then they entered boldly by faith. They would meet the same obstacles and fears that were there 40-years earlier. However, they went with the strength and courage that comes to those who walk by faith and not by sight.

We can do the same today if we walk by true faith and not by sight. When we have thoughts and ideas we need to determine if they are from the Lord or not. Let us filter them through the faith filter by asking the key question, "Am I trusting the Lord or myself?"

Thus far we have examined four filters for discerning our thoughts and intentions. Let us apply these in our decisions in life.

The Seven Filters

Filter #1 – Am I living like a spiritual person?

Filter # 2 – Does God's word say it is ok?

Filter #3 – Are my methods correct?

    (Am I seeking the right things the right way?)

    (Am I doing the right things the right way?)

Filter #4 – Am I trusting the Lord or myself?

Steven B. Hankins, Th.D.

Filter # 5 – What do other spiritual people think?

"for by wise guidance you can wage your war, and in abundance of counselors there is victory." (Proverbs 24:6, ESV)

In 1977, while serving in the United States Army in Germany, I had an interview to join the division staff as an aid to the assistant division commander. I thought it would be a great opportunity to see how a division level staff group functioned. At this level the planning of a military operation is done by a variety of military specialists. The planning involves specialists in operations, logistics, intelligence, supporting services and etcetera. The success is based largely on the contributions of each entity in the planning. Yet when it is all said and done the division commander makes the final determination regarding the operational plan.

The passage in Proverbs 24 has a military feel to it but the principles contained therein are not limited to military operations. They are truths that can be applied in any situation. It is especially useful in making decisions and filtering our thoughts. In this a *"multitude of counselors"* can make a huge difference and help keep us from acting upon impulses that might take us away from the purposes of God.

Good Counselors are Essential in Life

In Proverbs 24:3-7 we see two metaphors that prompt us to seek the counsel of others. They are of a person building and establishing a house and a general planning for war. Here we see some of the benefits of seeking godly counsel.

Good counselors provide wisdom and knowledge. – In the first metaphor we see two critical virtues that are necessary for success.

"By wisdom a house is built, and by understanding it is established; by knowledge the rooms are filled with all precious and pleasant riches" (Proverbs 24:3-4, ESV).

These virtues are wisdom and knowledge. We need both *"wisdom,"* referring to skill (Strong H2451), and *"knowledge"* in order to make good decisions. Both are virtues that we all lack to some extent. By God's grace the Holy Spirit continuously works to build up and completely furnish every believer's spiritual house with these two virtues. Yet because we are works in progress, we all still need help to make up for our deficiencies in *"wisdom"* and *"knowledge."* This is where godly counselors come in.

An example of this will be readily understood by any parent. When children are very young, they know very little and lack the skills necessary to negotiate life. The parent's role is extremely critical in these early stages of a child's development for two reasons. The first is to keep the child from dangerous situations. We lock up hazardous materials and medications so the child cannot touch or consume them. We hold their hands while crossing the street since they are not wise enough to watch out for traffic.

Second, parents have a responsibility to train up our children so they will mature in their ability to engage the issues of life correctly. Young children still need to develop in the knowledge of the hazards of life. We teach them not to take candy from strangers, etc. In a sense, the parents are the first line counselors for their children. Moreover, the parents work is never truly done. Even in the teen years the parents play an active role in the development of their adolescents. They need to guide, protect, and educate them in the new areas of life that they have not yet experienced. These are things like relationships, substances, seeking their first job, financial stewardship, etc.

In the same way as children need parents, new believers in Jesus need spiritual parents. When a person comes to faith in Christ, they are new creatures transformed by the power of God. Yet they are still babes in Christ (1 Cor 3:1). They lack much in knowledge and much in wisdom regarding how to live as a believer in a sin fallen world. They are not yet ready to be a spiritual counselor. They need a multitude of counselors.

I had a young single man who came to faith in Christ. He was in his twenties. He was saved and yet struggled in a lot of areas. He was trying to find his identity. He still had a lot of the world in him and he struggled with the temptations the world threw at him. One day he came to me for advice. He saw me as his counselor. He met a woman and apparently did something of which he was greatly ashamed. He did not give me the exact details but I perceived it to be something sexual. He did not know how this affected his spiritual life. He needed a counselor. He could have used one before the incident to keep him from this trouble and the pain of his guilt. However, now he needed one to help him through the process of restoration in his relationship with the Lord and to ease his own heart. He was a new creature in Christ who needed to grow in *"wisdom"* and *"knowledge."*

Do not think that because you have been a believer for a hundred years that you do not need the same. We all need spiritual people to whom we can go for advice. Even as the pastor of a church, I would regularly meet with other pastors to discuss issues and struggles that I was experiencing in the ministry. I would pick their brains for insight on various issues. We all need to be surrounded by spiritual people.

Good counselors provide safety. –The second metaphor has to do with a general planning for war. Planning for a battle is a major ordeal. To fail in planning will normally mean to fail in battle with disastrous results.

The Seven Filters

"*A wise man is full of strength, and a man of knowledge enhances his might, for by wise guidance you can wage your war, and in abundance of counselors there is victory.*" (Proverbs 24:5–6, ESV)

When I was in the military, we had an acronym characterized by five P's, "Prior Planning Prevents Poor Performance." For this reason, the commanding general will get as much expert advice as possible. Even generals seek the counsel of others.

The word translated as "*victory*" in the proverb can also be translated as deliverance or safety (Strong H8668). One thing we absolutely need when processing our thoughts is safety. There was a time in our world when government leaders who had to make critical decisions would call upon a pastor for advice and prayer. Those days seem to be fading away in the wind of change. No longer do people go to their spiritual leaders first. It should not be that way with believers but often it is.

When I did pre-marital counseling, I would always work to ensure the couple was equally yoked. Then I worked with the couple so they would understand the complexities of marriage and the lifelong commitment that they were making. I would tell them before the end of the counselling sessions to call me if they ever had any issues serious enough to have them contemplating divorce. I let them know that I would go out of my way sparing no expense to meet with them. Unfortunately, some of those marriages ended up in divorce and not one of the divorced couples ever contacted me. It is a problem of the age. Commitment is not commitment and seeking spiritual advice is ignored.

Using the filter of seeking godly counsel will save people from making poor decisions and subsequent suffering. Those seeking godly counsel will need to do the extra work involved with finding good counselors. They will need to set up appointments and meet with the counselors. Once they meet with the counselor, they must listen to the advice given with an open mind. It takes extra effort to seek godly counsel but the extra effort is well worth it.

Steven B. Hankins, Th.D.

Essential Practices in Using Counselors

Those seeking to filter out their thoughts and ideas to ensure they conform to the will of God need the filter of using godly counselors. There are some essential practices that the one seeking counsel must consider.

In Proverbs 24:7 we see a warning for all people. It is applicable to all who need evaluate their thoughts and ideas to ensure they conform to the will of God. *"Wisdom is too high for a fool; in the gate he does not open his mouth"* (Proverbs 24:7, ESV). In this verse we have a picture of elders sitting at the gate of the city and giving advice or judgment to those who will seek it. These elders were the wise men of the city. They were the counselors who were qualified to give their judgement on issues. The verse indicates that the *"fool"* has a problem. The *"fool"* is one who does not have the *"wisdom"* he seeks. This is obvious. However, the *"fool"* is also one who will not heed the wisdom given. The *"fool"* may not seek the right kind of counsel and even if received will not heed the advice given. To avoid being the *"fool"* there are several essential practices for using counselors.

One seeking godly counsel must be humble enough to listen. – One time, I was trying very hard to help a person in his job performance. I had some years of experience in the same job and thought I could shed some light on his work by giving him some constructive criticism. When I would give some godly counsel, he would always be polite by saying he appreciated my advice. However, it was kind of like "Yea, yea." He never seemed to do anything with the advice I gave him. This is often the problem that makes counselling ineffective. A wise person will not just listen to a counselor but also harken to the counsel given.

Pride in the heart of the person using the filter is normally the major issue. Granted, if the person seeking wisdom from a counselor used the first filter pride would not be an issue. The reason is that if those seeking counsel passed through the first filter, "Am I living like a spiritual person," they would not be struggling with the fleshly problem of pride. Yet pride remains a constant battle for every believer, even for the mature.

I had a leader in one church I pastored who thought he was quite a mature believer. On one occasion we were discussing an idea he had. In that discussion he went to great lengths to tell me he how he was not at all proud. That struck me as a problem. It has been my experience that anyone who boasts about not being proud has stumbled in his own opinion of himself. The person seeking counsel must understand the deceptive nature of pride and how it can destroy wise counsel.

The Scripture states, *"Pride goes before destruction, and a haughty spirit before a fall"* (Proverbs 16:18, ESV). Proud people will struggle to filter out their thoughts to ensure they align with the will of God. One of the problems I have seen with those seeking counsel is that they will often summarily reject the advice given. The writer of Proverbs wrote, *"A scoffer seeks wisdom in vain, but knowledge is easy for a man of understanding"* (Proverbs 14:6, ESV). Proud people who need *"wisdom"* may go to a counselor but will generally interpret the counsel in accordance with their own fleshly perceptions. They have a pride constructed filter that takes the advice of a godly counselor and removes anything that does not agree with their own preconceived ideas.

I had a couple come to me for marital counselling one time. I thought that both the man and the woman wanted to work out their issues. So, I spent time with them covering some of the major issues in marriages and how to deal with them. After that first meeting I discovered that one of them had no intention of reconciling their issues. He only wanted me to condone a divorce. He filtered out all the biblical counsel to arrive at his own preconceived desire, which was for divorce. The couple ended up divorcing and I spent time counseling his wife to help her deal with the emotional trauma of the divorce. This woman's husband displayed all the characteristics of a proud *"fool"* in seeking biblical counsel.

To use the filter of godly counselors those seeking *"wisdom"* must be living like spiritual people should and guard against their own wants and desires. Before meeting with a counselor, they should spend time in prayer asking the Lord to reveal any fleshly and prideful preconceptions that they might have on an issue. They should ask for the Lord give them an open mind. In the session they should listen to and prayerfully consider the advice given. They should also examine the Scriptures to see if the advice is correct. The Berean Christians set the example in this as they examined what Paul preached to see if it was true according to the Scriptures (Acts 17:11).

One seeking godly counsel must choose godly counselors. – Counselors who are not living like a spiritual person present a major issue. In the ministry I have seen many that have chosen foolish counselors. The writer of Proverbs stated, *"One who is wise is cautious and turns away from evil, but a fool is reckless and careless"* (Proverbs 14:16, ESV). One must be careful in selecting counselors. There are certain things that one should seek in a counselor. The overriding characteristic is that the counselor must be a spiritual person who is living like a spiritual person should live. The counselor must be a Spirit filled person who is seeking the Lord. What are some of the qualities one should see in this type of person? There are many but here are some of the most prominent.

Choose a mature versus an immature counselor. – Too often people choose immature believers when seeking spiritual advice. The problem is that the immature believer lacks the wisdom that comes with spiritual growth. The wisdom that comes from spiritual maturity is essential for giving wise advice. We have a prime example of this in Israel as Solomon's son Rehoboam assumed the kingship of the nation (2 Chr 10).

After Rehoboam assumed kingship a contingency from the northern part of the kingdom met with him. They asked him to lighten the load of labor and taxation that was upon them. Rehoboam took counsel with the old men who had served Solomon and they gave him this advice. *"If you will be good to this people and please them and speak good words to them, then they will be your servants forever*" (2 Chronicles 10:7, ESV). However, he ignored the advice of the older mature men and sought the counsel of the young men who grew up with him. The young men gave him this advice.

> *"Thus shall you speak to the people who said to you, 'Your father made our yoke heavy, but you lighten it for us'; thus shall you say to them, 'My little finger is thicker than my father's thighs. And now, whereas my father laid on you a heavy yoke, I will add to your yoke. My father disciplined you with whips, but I will discipline you with scorpions.'"* (2 Chronicles 10:10–11, ESV)

What did Rehoboam do? He rejected the advice of the old men who had wisdom and took the advice of the young men. He spoke harshly to the people, which resulted in a rebellion within the nation. This divided the nation in two, the northern kingdom called Israel and the southern called Judah. The two kingdoms never reunited. Following the advice of immature counselors caused a permanent problem for the nation. Likewise, following the advice of an immature person can cause great problems for anyone trying to filter out their thoughts and ideas to ensure they align with the will of God.

I was serving in a church one time and ran into this example. There was a nice young couple in the church and the man's wife was out of town on a mini-vacation. While she was gone her husband had eyes for one of the single girls in the congregation. He thought she was nice and wanted to know if he should approach her for a date. So, he went to one of his close friends and asked him what to do. His friend was another young Christian in the church. His friend told him that he should go for it. Thus, he began seeing the single girl while the wife was away. When his wife got back from vacation, she discovered what was going on and became very upset. Of course, the rumors were already spreading. The actions of the man were incorrect and hurtful to his wife and to others in the congregation who knew about it. Another deacon and I spent considerable energy counselling the man, his wife, and the girl the man was dating in order to bring restoration and settle the situation. We also had to speak to everyone who knew about what went on. All this could have been avoided if the man would have sought mature godly counsel.

Whenever you have a thought or idea regarding something, pass it through the filter of a godly mature counselor. Always seek a counselor who displays spiritual maturity. Avoid or seriously scrutinize any advice given by a spiritually immature person. You want counselors who have been in the faith for a considerable time and have displayed a life of devotion to the Lord. If you do not have one speak with the pastor of your church.

Choose an honest versus a patronizing counselor. – Unfortunately, there are many counselors who will tell you what you want to hear rather than what you need to know. This is another deceptive trap that will take one off track when it comes to discerning one's thoughts and ideas.

We see an example of this in the account of Ahab king of Israel and Jehoshaphat king of Judah, when they were considering war against Syria (2 Chronicles 18). As they considered war Jehoshaphat asked Ahab to seek some prophets who might give counsel regarding the situation. Then Ahab gathered 400 prophets and asked them.

> *"Shall we go to battle against Ramoth-gilead, or shall I refrain?"* they answered him, *"Go up, for God will give it into the hand of the king"* (2 Chronicles 18:5, ESV).

Yet Jehoshaphat was not satisfied and asked if there was another prophet. Ahab stated that there was one, *"Micaiah the son of Imlah"* (2 Chronicles 18:7, ESV). However, Ahab did not want his counsel and gave this reason, *"I hate him, for he never prophesies good concerning me, but always evil"* (2 Chronicles 18:7, ESV). Can you see the problem here? Ahab wanted prophets who would tell him the good things that he wanted to hear. As a result, he established a counselling network that filtered out the truth.

The Seven Filters

At Jehoshaphat's request they sent messengers to Micaiah. The messengers told Micaiah that the 400 prophets spoke favorably to the king and that he should do the same. Micaiah responded, *"As the LORD lives, what my God says, that I will speak"* (2 Chronicles 18:13, ESV). When Micaiah spoke to the king, he at first jested with the king by giving him an assurance of victory but then told him the truth. The Lord revealed to Micaiah that Israel would be soundly defeated in battle (2 Chr 18:16, 19). He further told Ahab of his vision and stated that Ahab would be enticed to fall in battle through a lying spirit in the mouths of the 400 prophets (2 Chronicles 18:20-22). It happened just as the true prophet of the Lord had said. Ahab died in battle and Israel was defeated.

What was the major problem here? Ahab always chose counselors who would tell him what he wanted to hear. Moreover, when the only true prophet spoke, he would not listen. It is often like this with people choosing a counselor. In the example of the man who decided to date a girl in the congregation while his wife was gone, he chose a close friend as the counselor. This counselling was doomed from the start. First the person he asked was an immature believer and second, he was a friend.

True friends who are mature Christians will generally tell you the truth even it is difficult. However, even mature Christians may have a strong temptation, because of the friendship, to soften the message or tell you what you want to hear. Try to avoid choosing a close friend as a counselor to help you sort through your thoughts and ideas. If you feel your pastor or counsellor is your close friend, make sure to preface your problem with something like this, "I want to hear the truth from you even if you do not think it is what I want to hear."

When you choose a counselor find one who will be honest with you. You do not want counselors who will tell you what you want to hear. You want sound biblical counsel. A good counselor will tell the truth in love.

Choose a righteous versus an unrighteous counselor. – This should go without saying. If you choose a counselor who is a spiritual person living as a spiritual person should live, the one you choose will be a righteous person. In the Bible we have many examples of unrighteous counselors.

One such example of an unrighteous counselor is seen during the reign of king Ahaziah of the Southern Kingdom, Judah. His mother Athaliah, the daughter of Ahab the king of the Northern Kingdom, counseled him in following the ways of evil. As a result, we see that Ahaziah *"also walked in the ways of the house of Ahab, for his mother was his counselor in doing wickedly"* (2 Chronicles 22:3, ESV). Thus, he brought the apostasy of the northern kingdom Israel into the southern kingdom Judah. The text further states that he followed his father's counselors *"to his destruction"* (2 Chronicles 22:4, KJV). It ends up that Ahaziah joined his uncle Joram in a campaign against Syria and was wounded in the battle. Wounded, he returned to Jezreel to recover which was a fatal decision. There he was put to death by Jehu who was anointed by Elisha to destroy Ahab's descendants (2 Ki 9:1-29).

The point is this. There are some out there who will intentionally counsel a person to follow a path that is contrary to the will of God. They are unrighteous counselors. There are certain Christian sects following progressive ideologies. They believe that certain sexual practices forbidden by the word of God are fine in today's culture. They believe that killing the unborn child is fine. Some of these believe that there are many ways to heaven. Unrighteous counselling may come from counselors professing high qualifications. Beware of the counselors you select.

When I was pastoring in New Hampshire we had a couple join us for worship who had stumbled into the Unitarian Universalist Church the week before. They were trying to find us and stopped there to ask for directions. When they did, the response they received was something like this, "Oh, those people. They focus too much on the Bible." That was a great testimony for our church but a condemning thought for so many groups that are trying to guide people.

When you look for a counselor make sure you select one who will counsel you in righteousness. This will be a person who is seeking God and His righteousness and who will give sound biblical advice.

Choose a multitude of good counselors. – The writer of Proverbs indicated that having more than one counsellor is preferable. He stated, *"for by wise guidance you can wage your war, and in abundance of counselors there is victory"* (Proverbs 24:6, ESV). The saying goes, "Two heads are better than one." It is a truth reinforced in the Scriptures.

I was on a business trip to a major city one time with a group of people. After checking into the hotel, we asked the concierge for a good place to have dinner. He gave us a place and said it was about two blocks away. Then he asked us if we wanted a taxi. We said, "No, it is close so we will just walk." He advised that we take a taxi and then told us that if we were to walk there, we should stay in a large group. The problem was that getting to the restaurant that was only two blocks away meant that we had to walk through a bad part of town. So, we walked there together for safety. The point I am making is that there is safety in numbers. It is the same way in getting help in discerning our thoughts and ideas. The more counselors, godly ones, with whom we can speak the better we will do in using this filter.

On a couple occasions I was on a team training exercise where we were asked the order of importance of certain items if stranded on a desert island or similar place. The correct order was put together by experts in survival. After doing the exercise individually we were broken into teams to repeat the exercise as a team. Generally, the teams had six or more participants. In every case the teams did better in getting the order correct than any one individual. The point was to show us the power of getting multiple inputs and viewpoints in sorting out issues.

The writer of Ecclesiastes highlights this truth that people working together will prevail and do better than an individual alone.

> *"Two are better than one, because they have a good reward for their toil . . . And though a man might prevail against one who is alone, two will withstand him—a threefold cord is not quickly broken."* (Ecclesiastes 4:9, 12, ESV)

He tells us that people working together will have a *"good reward"* for what they are doing. The word translated *"reward,"* *sakar*, can also be translated as salary or payment (Strong H7939). It pays to use a multitude of godly counselors when seeking to sort out one's thoughts and ideas to ensure they are in alignment with the will of God.

Now in practice it would be great to get all the counselors in one room at one time. In some situations, like when a church is seeking to begin a new work or vision, this is easy. One of the things I did in recasting the vision in my last church was to put a twelve-person team together to go through a year-long process of seeking the Lord's will for the church. The process worked exceptionally well and we did establish an awesome vision that the entire congregation embraced. It was a lot of work but it paid off.

Unfortunately, is it not usually possible to get all one's counsellors together at in one place at the same time. Generally, it will require sitting down with a variety of individuals on different occasions. This will take more time and effort but it is worth it. For in receiving input from a multitude of counselors one will get a variety of thoughts and viewpoints. The combination of these will provide a more complete picture, which will contribute to making better decisions.

Personal Responsibility for Action

One of my first jobs after leaving the military was to work as a project engineer in research and development in a paper converting corporation. One of the projects I had was to have another engineer assist me in determining what to do with several rolls of paper that would not function in one of the printing presses. After analyzing the process and the paper we concluded that the paper was defective. So, I wrote the report, signed it, and turned it over to my boss. He read it and immediately called me into his office and read me the riot act. He was not happy with the conclusion because we decided to write off the cost of the bad paper, which was a lot of money.

As I sat with the boss in this excruciating meeting, he kept asking me if the conclusion was influenced by the other engineer who had more time with the company than I did. He even kept saying he did not know why I was covering for the other engineer. I could have easily said that the other guy influenced me but I did not. It was my project, I wrote the report, and I signed it. I took responsibility for the project and I made the decision to publish the conclusion.

This illustrates a point. When we make decisions, we are personally responsible for those decisions. After getting advice from a multitude of counselors, believers must understand that they are personally responsible for the decisions they make in response to the advice given. No one can blame the counsellor for their input. Paul addressed this point when he wrote to the Romans regarding making decisions in questionable areas (Romans 14). It is a sobering statement.

> *"we will all stand before the judgment seat of God; for it is written, 'As I live, says the Lord, every knee shall bow to me, and every tongue shall confess to God.' So then each of us will give an account of himself to God."* (Romans 14:10–12, ESV)

Paul presented the fact that every person will have to give an account to God for their own decisions. The word translated as *"judgment seat,"* *bema*, refers to an elevated step, a tribunal throne (Thayer p31). It is not to be confused with the *"great white throne"* final judgment of the unbeliever (Rev 20:11-15). Paul referred to the place where the believer's works will be judged (2 Cor 5:10) for either reward or loss thereof (2 Cor 3:10-15). Believers are personally responsible for the actions they take in response to their thought and ideas. In other words, we cannot blame others for the decisions we make. We will all give an account for the things we do in the body.

Sometimes we may receive counsel from one person that misses the mark. We must remember that the final decision on what to do with our thoughts and ideas is up to us. Moreover, we are personally responsible to the Lord for our choices.

Years ago, I was called to plant a church in Savannah. We had a glorious start. The entire ministry was focused on reaching dorm students on the local college campus. Things went exceptionally well, at least for a few years. We grew rapidly and then began experiencing some difficulty. The growth just kind of stopped. Each year we would see students leave and a new crop enter. Honestly, I became a bit discouraged and was looking for direction. I went to a couple counsellors who sought to encourage me. They suggested that I see one of the longest tenured Baptist pastors in our city who had a large church.

So, I went to see the pastor of this church to get his advice. We talked for a while. Then he told me, since my undergraduate degree and most of my professional experience was in engineering and manufacturing, that he did not believe I could succeed in the pastorate. His view was that technical people were not skilled to do such a task. I was devastated and puzzled after hearing his comments. He was the only one of the counselors who suggested anything like this. All the others were supportive. Yet he was touted as the one to have all the answers and seemed to have the most experience.

Leaving his office, I was quite perplexed. I left with my head hung down and my tail between my legs. At home I sulked for a while, contemplated shutting down our little church, and going back to full time in engineering. I even had ample opportunities to do so. However, after much prayer and contemplation I just could

The Seven Filters

not give up the calling to the ministry. I believed with all my heart that the Lord would have me continue the pastoral work. At the "*bema of Christ*" I was not going to be able to say that I left the calling because one man gave me such counsel. We will never be able to blame others for the decisions we make. They are ours and we are personally responsible.

So, what are we to do in using the filter, "What do other spiritual people have to say?" We are to select spiritual and godly people who are living as a spiritual people should to help us in our decisions. We should select multiple people like this since in a multitude of counselors there is safety. We must listen to all these counselors without preconceived ideas regarding what we want to do. Then having heard what they have advised we must pray to the Lord for wisdom. After this we pass our ideas through the last two filters prior to making a final decision. Moreover, through this process we always remember that we are personally responsible for the decisions we make.

Filter #1 – Am I living like a spiritual person?

Filter # 2 – Does God's word say it is ok?

Filter #3 – Are my methods correct?

(Am I seeking and doing the right things the right way?)

Filter #4 – Am I trusting the Lord or myself?

Filter #5 - What do other spiritual people think?

Filter # 6 – Is my motive to glorify God alone?

"So, whether you eat or drink, or whatever you do, do all to the glory of God."
(1 Corinthians 10:31, ESV)

When my brother and I were in grade school we had an interesting opportunity. My dad purchased a little tool for removing dandelions from the yard. He wanted all the dandelions gone. He told us, "I'll give you five cents for every dandelion that you pull up correctly and show me." While dad was inside watching the Philadelphia Phillies playing baseball, we went to town picking up the dandelions.

A good time later we told our dad that we were done. He came outside to count the dandelions and when he saw the box full of them, he exclaimed, "Where in the heck did you get all those dandelions?" We told him, "Well, after we got done in our yard, we went to the neighbors' yards and got all of theirs." He did not seem a hundred percent pleased with our entrepreneurship but settled anyway. He figured we would each make a dollar or so each. Instead, we had much more.

The moral of the story is this. Yes, we wanted to please our dad. After all he just wanted a better-looking yard. However, we had an ulterior motive. That was to make money. Our motives for picking the dandelions moved my brother and I to do something that was not in the will of my father.

Motives are important. Often when we get thoughts or ideas to do something our motives can get out of order. Filter number six for discerning our thoughts and ideas is the motive check. We must ask the question, "Is my motive to glorify God alone?"

Man's Chief End in Life

When we come to Filter #6, we arrive at the filter of purpose. What is the chief purpose for man's existence? The Westminster Shorter Catechism has as its first question, "What is the chief end of man?" Its answer is, "Man's chief end is to glorify God and enjoy him forever." (Westminster Pg. 2)

Paul wrote to the Corinthians regarding the issue of Christian liberty in the area of eating meat sacrificed to idols (1 Cor 10:23-33). In this section he presented a universal truth regarding the filter of motives. He stated in *"whatever you do, do all to the glory of God."* Our chief end in life to glorify God must be our prime motivation in everything. This is a critical filter for discerning our thoughts and ideas to ensure they align with the will of God. God will never prompt us to do anything that will miss the mark of bringing glory to Him.

Glorifying God in everything is not a mere suggestion. In 1 Corinthians 10:31 the verb *"do"* is a present tense command, which means that we must seek to continuously bring glory and honor to God. It is true that there are times when we miss the mark in this area due to those impetuous moments when we sin. I struggle on occasion with traffic on the highways, especially when someone cuts me off or will not show the common courtesy of letting me merge. In those times my thoughts and even my responses are not always glorifying to God. Of course, having bad thoughts towards others does not characterize my life. Christ and His righteousness are what define me as a believer. When I do sin, I have the promise of God's cleansing through confession (1 John 1:9). Then along with confession I purpose in my heart to try very hard to *"walk by the Spirit"* and not repeat my failure. For I know that my transgression has not glorified God.

The Scriptures command us to glorify God in all our thoughts, our words, and our actions. This is our principal duty and this motive to glorify God becomes a paramount filter for our thoughts and ideas.

Steven B. Hankins, Th.D.

Results of Improper Motives

When our motives are wrong, we open ourselves to deception and are unable to make the best choices with regards to our thoughts and ideas. One of the great problems we see in proper motivation is that of self-glorification.

Self-glorification creates difficulties in life. – One of the greatest examples of self-glorification is seen in the life of King Nebuchadnezzar of Babylon who reigned from 605-562 B.C. Nebuchadnezzar was a successful military leader and was instrumental in orchestrating many building activities in Babylon. Under his reign Babylon had conquered vast territories. This included the destruction of Jerusalem in 586 B.C. in which he took a remnant of the Jews captive and deported them by foot to Babylon. However, all of Nebuchadnezzar's successes fed a prideful heart that led to his own degradation.

Following the Lord's miraculous deliverance of three Hebrew men, Shadrach, Meshach, and Abednego from the fiery furnace, Nebuchadnezzar praised the *"Most High God"* for all the works God did for the king (Dan 3:8-4:3). Yet this same one who praised the God of the Hebrew men would later stumble in a sin of self-exaltation.

Following the Lord's deliverance of the three Hebrew men, Nebuchadnezzar had a dream that scared him. He called upon the wise men of the Chaldeans to interpret the dream but they could not (Dan 4:4-7). After *"the magicians, the enchanters, the Chaldeans, and the astrologers"* failed to interpret the dream, one of the deportees named Daniel arrived (Daniel 4:7-8). Nebuchadnezzar relayed the dream to him for interpretation (Dan 4:5-18).

The dream was of a large strong and towering tree that reached to heaven. It was visible to the whole earth and it was beautiful. It gave shade to the beasts of the field and a resting place for the birds of the air. It also provided the nourishment for all flesh. However, a holy one came down from heaven and proclaimed the tree would be chopped down, the branches lopped

The Seven Filters

off, the leaves removed, and its fruit scattered. Moreover, the beasts of the field and the birds of the air were to flee. The stump of the tree was to be bound. The holy one from heaven then referred to the stump as a person who would have his place with the beasts of the field and have a beast's mind given to him for an extended time. The main point of the dream was revealed to the king. It was so all would know the supreme sovereign authority of God over all.

> *"that the living may know that the Most High rules the kingdom of men and gives it to whom he will and sets over it the lowliest of men"* (Daniel 4:17, ESV).

Daniel then interpreted the dream for Nebuchadnezzar (Dan 4:19-27). The tree represented the king and the greatness of his kingdom. The decree of chopping down the tree, the scattering of its fruit, the flight of the living creatures, the binding of the stump, and its representation of the man given over to be like a beast was given as a message of warning to the king. Daniel gave Nebuchadnezzar the interpretation of the dream that explained what would happen to the king.

> *"this is the interpretation, O king: It is a decree of the Most High, which has come upon my lord the king, that you shall be driven from among men, and your dwelling shall be with the beasts of the field. You shall be made to eat grass like an ox, and you shall be wet with the dew of heaven, and seven periods of time shall pass over you, till you know that the Most High rules the kingdom of men and gives it to whom he will."* (Daniel 4:24–25, ESV)

Then Daniel gave a word of exhortation to the king to repent from his sins, to practice righteousness, and to show mercy to the oppressed. In doing so the king would have the possibility of extending his reign of prosperity.

However, the king forgot Daniel's exhortation (Dan 4:27-33). Twelve months later while the king was on the roof of the palace, he made a great prideful blunder. Looking over his kingdom he stated, *"Is not this great Babylon, which I have built by my mighty power as a royal residence and for the glory of my majesty?"* (Daniel 4:30, ESV). In this statement Nebuchadnezzar stole the glory from God. It was the revelation of the king's sinful heart. As a result, just as Daniel had interpreted, the king was driven into the field, given the mind of a beast of the field, and made to eat grass like an ox. He lived like this for seven periods of time until his hair and fingernails grew long.

Following the seven periods of time Nebuchadnezzar regained his senses and gave glory to God (Dan 4:34-37).

"Now I, Nebuchadnezzar, praise and extol and honor the King of heaven, for all his works are right and his ways are just; and those who walk in pride he is able to humble" (Daniel 4:37, ESV).

Then once again he experienced the prosperity of his kingdom.

The point we must take from the account of Nebuchadnezzar is this. Self-glorification is to steal the glory from God and those that do so fall into a serious trap. The writer of Proverbs put it like this, *"Pride goes before destruction, and a haughty spirit before a fall"* (Proverbs 16:18, ESV). We will never be able to accurately filter out our thoughts and ideas to make sure they align with the will of God if we allow prideful attitudes to result in self-glorification.

You say, "Yea, I get it." Yet how many times have we failed to give glory to God? How many times have we boasted, "Look what I have done." We will never be able to use the filter, "Is my motive to glorify God alone?" if we are not giving the glory to God in our heart. Thus, everyone seeking to determine if their thoughts and intentions align with the will of God need to take a time of serious self-examination regarding their motives. This has been mentioned before but needs repeating. We should pray the prayer of the Psalmist.

"Search me, O God, and know my heart! Try me and know my thoughts! And see if there be any grievous way in me, and lead me in the way everlasting!" (Psalm 139:23–24, ESV)

Self-promotion in life results in lost eternal reward. – One of the large problems that I have seen in Christian circles is that of believers seeking an audience so that people will praise them. Let us face it. People do need affirmation. Yet seeking affirmation is a trap that can lead to self-promotion. Jesus spoke about this in the Sermon on the Mount.

> *"Beware of practicing your righteousness before other people in order to be seen by them, for then you will have no reward from your Father who is in heaven. Thus, when you give to the needy, sound no trumpet before you, as the hypocrites do in the synagogues and in the streets, that they may be praised by others. Truly, I say to you, they have received their reward."* (Matthew 6:1–2, ESV)

> *"And when you pray, you must not be like the hypocrites. For they love to stand and pray in the synagogues and at the street corners, that they may be seen by others. Truly, I say to you, they have received their reward."* (Matthew 6:5, ESV)

> *"And when you fast, do not look gloomy like the hypocrites, for they disfigure their faces that their fasting may be seen by others. Truly, I say to you, they have received their reward."* (Matthew 6:16, ESV)

In each one of these warnings, we see a similar theme. Those who do good works with a motivation to be seen by others will miss out on heavenly reward. Jesus stated that they who receive glory from men on earth have already received their reward. You might think that this is limited to those Pharisees, the hypocrites of Jesus' day, and not to people in the church context. However, this happens in the church today with great regularity. It is a subtle trap for us preachers as it is trap for every believer.

My first exposure to this was in a small church. In this church we always had special music. This is where people of the congregation who felt they had some sort of musical talent would get up before the congregation and sing something that was supposed to be appropriate. On one occasion we had a man with a good voice, he could sing. However, in one service he started his special by sitting on the platform with his back leaning against the podium. Then he swung around facing the congregation and stood up. One parishioner commented that he was doing his best Perry Como (a pop artist from the 40's and 50s) impersonation. It was like we were watching a nightclub act. The problem was that his presentation was not drawing people to worship God but to focus on himself. His work of singing was done to be seen by others.

I have watched as members of worship teams in more contemporary churches have sought to put on the cool vibe where the music had more of a concert feel than that of worship. Once I spoke for an organization in a church that had people get up on the platform and give testimony only to see young people force a display that seemed disingenuous. There are prayer meetings where certain people will focus on making the most flowery prayers so that others would view them as the most spiritual of people. I think you get the point.

From personal experience I know how easy it is to fall into the trap of doing good works to gain the attention of others. I venture to say that many a preacher has stood on the platform and preached wondering if people liked what he said for the wrong reason. How many times do preachers revel in the glory of their church growth? One of the first questions I usually heard at pastors' conferences was, "How big is your congregation?" I have run into many parishioners who have sought to be teachers so they would be highly regarded by others.

The problem with the attitude of self-promotion is that it steals the glory from God. For this reason, it is a motive that will ultimately bring failure at the time of the believer's reward. As Paul wrote, there is a time coming when every believer will stand at the judgment seat of Christ.

> "*For we must all appear before the judgment seat of Christ, so that each one may receive what is due for what he has done in the body, whether good or evil*" (2 Corinthians 5:10, ESV).

This judgement of believers is not one for condemnation but for reward. The believer will either be rewarded or suffer loss of

The Seven Filters

reward (1 Cor 3:12-15). The good work is that which brings glory and honor to God. These are the good works that will result in reward. Those works that were focused on self-glorification will miss the mark and suffer loss.

So, we must do good works for one purpose as Jesus stated, *"let your light shine before others, so that they may see your good works and give glory to your Father who is in heaven"* (Matthew 5:16, ESV). Works done with the wrong motivation of self-glorification will interfere with the believer's capacity to use this filter in discerning one's thoughts and ideas. The remedy for this problem is confession, repentance, and prayer for God's abundant grace.

Ways That Glorify God

Understanding that we have a command to glorify God the question becomes, "In what ways do we do this?" The word *"glory,"* *doxa*, is very wide in application. It has to do with glory, dignity, honor, praise, and worship (Strong G1391). Considering this definition, the thoughts and ideas that are of God will drive our actions to glorify, dignify, honor, praise, and worship Him. This involves the totality of our time and our actions. Let us consider some specifics regarding how this works.

Doing everything in the name of Jesus glorifies God. – In this issue of motives, we previously discussed that the believer's primary motive was to glorify God. We saw this from Paul's exhortation, *"So, whether you eat or drink, or whatever you do, do all to the glory of God"* (1 Corinthians 10:31, ESV). We see a similar thought in Colossians where Paul wrote a similar exhortation.

> *"And whatever you do, in word or deed, do everything in the name of the Lord Jesus, giving thanks to God the Father through him"* (Colossians 3:17, ESV).

Thus, there is a direct association between giving glory to God in everything we do and doing everything in the name of Jesus.

One problem with this is that few Christians understand what it means to do something in the name of Jesus. We often tag every prayer with the phrase, "In the name of Jesus. Amen." I am afraid that it may become a meaningless mantra for some, becoming just something said to end a prayer. We must consider the depth of what we are saying when we invoke the name of Jesus. To invoke the name of Jesus without knowing Him can lead to missing the will of God and emptiness in prayer. Likewise, to misunderstand what it means to do things in the name of Jesus can result in believers missing the mark with respect to God's will. In the extreme case it can be disastrous.

In a conference I once attended the speaker highlighted the problem of invoking the name of Jesus in an empty way. He brought to our attention the record of the seven sons of Sceva in Ephesus (Acts 19:11-20). In Ephesus, the Lord was working mightily through Paul. Many mighty works were being done in physical and spiritual healings. Apparently the seven sons of Sceva had observed or heard of the works of Paul in delivering people from evil spirits. So, these itinerant Jewish exorcists set out to do the same. Luke recorded that they "*undertook to invoke the name of the Lord Jesus over those who had evil spirits, saying, 'I adjure you by the Jesus whom Paul proclaims'*" (Acts 19:13, ESV). We must consider what resulted from their effort. The record continues, "*the evil spirit answered them, 'Jesus I know, and Paul I recognize, but who are you?'*" (Acts 19:15, ESV). Then the man who had the evil spirit leaped on the seven, overpowered them, and gave them a good going over, causing them to flee naked and wounded. What was the seven sons' problem? They invoked the name of one they did not know.

Many in the world today invoke the name of a Savior that they really do not know. Too often even true believers invoke the name of Jesus without giving any thought to the weight of His glorious name and what it means.

It should be easy for us to understand what doing something in the name of Jesus means if we bring this down to something familiar in the earthly realm. What would it mean if we did

The Seven Filters

something in the name of a friend, family member, or neighbor? One time we were in the process of purchasing a home and I had to be in Germany for a trade show at the time of the closing. So, I had a "Limited Power of Attorney" created for my wife to transact all matters that I needed to do in the purchase of the home. In other words, she was using my authority to execute things according to my will in the purchase of the home. Using this "Limited Power of Attorney" meant that she could only wield my power on the things I specified using the funds that I authorized for the purpose of purchasing the home.

Similarly, to do something in the name of Jesus implies that we are doing something by His authority granted to us for the purpose of accomplishing His will. Thus, we could never pray for or do something in His name that violated His supreme sovereign purposes. In prayer we could never pray in the name of Jesus to have success in robbing a bank. We could never rob a bank in Jesus' name. However, in His name we can pray or do things that align with His will. Moreover, we are blessed to do His will by His power working within us, with us, and through us (Phil 4:13).

This command to *"do everything in the name of the Lord Jesus"* is given in the context of our new position, identity, and life in Christ (Col 3:1-17). Everything we do as believers must be done in the name of Jesus and in doing so, we will bring glory and honor to God.

Setting our minds on and seeking those things which are heavenly glorifies God. – In Colossians 3:1-2 Paul exhorts us to *"seek the things that are above"* and to set our *"minds on the things that are above."* I have often heard the expression, "Some people are so heavenly minded that they are no earthly good." Here Paul's exhortation contradicts this statement. These exhortations are again present tense commands, which indicates we are to continuously be heavenly minded. Perhaps if we were properly minded towards heavenly things, we would be more actively engaged in displaying the virtues of heaven in our lives today. In doing so we would make a greater impact in the world around us for God's glory.

I do get what people mean when they say, "Some people are so heavenly minded that they are no earthly good." I know of people that spend all day in the Bible, watching Christian programming, and reading Christian materials. All this is great. However, often these same people who have a massive intake of Christian content do virtually nothing outside of their little holy confines to reflect the glory of God in a dark world. These people are the ones "so heavenly minded that they are no earthly good." Jesus gave all believers the clear command to let their light so shine that people would see their good works and glorify God (Matt 5:16). If we are going to glorify God in what we do, we must be heavenly minded. However, our heavenly mindedness must result in good works.

From the standpoint of filtering out the thoughts and ideas that are outside the will of God we must have a heavenly viewpoint. How does our heavenly citizenship influence our motives? Are we seeking to glorify our Heavenly Father?

Putting to death the former ways and putting on the new glorifies God. – In Colossians 3:5-17 Paul presented principles regarding the removal of the former ways and replacing them with the new in a believer's life. He began with these words, *"Put to death therefore what is earthly in you."* Unfortunately, all believers living on this earth are still influenced by the flesh, the world system, and spiritual forces of evil. These things are constantly working to get us off track and do the things that we should not. Paul's solution is to put to death the things contrary to the kingdom of heaven in us. In other words, we must examine ourselves and reject those things contrary to righteousness.

Paul then went on to explain a principle that is akin to changing clothing.

> *"put off the old self with its practices and have put on the new self, which is being renewed in the knowledge after the image of its creator"* (Colossians 3:9-10, ESV).

It is interesting that Paul spoke in the past tense, which indicates that we have already *"put off the old"* and *"put on the new."* The word *"put off,"* *apekdomai*, means to wholly put off (Strong G554) and *"put on,"* *enduo*, refers to sinking into a garment (Strong G1746). The imagery Paul used is one of the believers having already changed their clothes.

I have worked in some very dirty places in my life. While working on servicing printing machinery I would often be covered with grease, ink, and assorted grime. At the end of the day, I would have to get back on an airplane and travel home. Yet I was so filthy that I knew there was no way anyone would let me on the airplane or at least they should not have. So, I would go into the plant locker-room wash up and put on clean clothes. When I got on the airplane people would not see the formerly grimy field service person that I was just an hour earlier. They would see a completely different person.

When the Lord saved us, He changed us. The old unrighteous garments came off and we were clothed with new righteous garments, the righteousness of Jesus. Yet we have two huge struggles. First, we still struggle with the old nature, the flesh (Gal 5:16-17). Second, we live in a corrupted world where its sinful influences are strong and often rub off on us (Rom 12:2). As a result, our spiritual clothing often does not radiate as brightly as it should. Thus, Paul commanded that every believer endeavor to display these righteous garments in everyday life. *"Put on then, as God's chosen ones, holy and beloved, compassionate hearts, kindness, humility, meekness, and patience,"* (Colossians 3:12, ESV).

What does this heavenly clothing look like? Paul went on to describe this heavenly clothing with a description of its virtues in the subsequent verses (v12b-17). The list includes heartfelt compassion, kindness, humility, meekness, patience, forbearance, forgiveness, love, the rule of Christ's peace in our hearts, thankfulness, the richness of His word dwelling in us, giving loving exhortation, and having the joy of worship in our hearts. These are the virtues of the believer's spiritual clothing that should be displayed for all to see. If our motives are correct, they will include putting off the former ways of the world and the flesh, and endeavoring to wear the manifestation of Christ's righteousness in this darkened world.

Seeking the betterment of others glorifies God. – As previously mentioned in 1 Corinthians 10:23-33, Paul dealt with the issue of eating food sacrificed to idols. Paul understood that idols were nothing and could not affect food. However, one's perceptions or convictions were an issue. To this issue Paul indicated that we must be careful in the use of Christian liberty because it can have an adverse influence on another's conscience (v28-29). In this passage there are several key principles regarding our consideration of others.

One key issue is making sure our desire or motive is to build up others rather than to tear them down as Paul explained.

> *"'All things are lawful,' but not all things are helpful. 'All things are lawful,' but not all things build up. Let no one seek his own good, but the good of his neighbor"* (1 Corinthians 10:23–24, ESV).

The verb *"helpful,"* *sumphero*, literally means to bear together and could be translated profitable (Strong G4851). The verb *"build up,"* *oikodomeo*, literally has the idea of building a house. Paul indicated that while everything was lawful not everything might be good. The reason was because it was more important to be profitable towards another and to build one up than to exercise personal liberty and do the opposite.

This goes against the philosophy of the world system, which is every man for himself. A shift supervisor once worked for me who had a philosophy that he would make the other shifts look bad so that he would always look better even if his performance was mediocre. The result of this philosophy was poor morale and performance in the entire three shift workforce. This philosophy lacked teamwork. It lacked consideration of the other shifts. Many times, one shift would do the hard work that it took to set the next shift up for success. Yet because of this self-indulging attitude the shifts before this supervisor lost all incentive to do the hard work to make him a success. The entire manufacturing facility was in a downward spiral.

You say this could not happen in the church! However, I have seen it. Self-promotion in church members happens all the time. I met a pastor once who flaunted the use of his Christian liberty regarding the use of alcoholic beverages in front of other believers without regards to their personal convictions on the matter. This type of behavior does not glorify God because it can tear others down instead of building them up.

Seeking the betterment of others is not an easy work. It is not one undertaken by the proud. It is difficult and requires self-sacrifice. Yet it is worth it. The motivation to glorify God must include a view that sees the importance of others. Paul wrote, *"Do nothing from selfish ambition or conceit, but in humility count others more significant than yourselves"* (Philippians 2:3, ESV).

Worshipping in spirit and truth glorifies God. – When Jesus met the Samaritan woman at the well, He presented insight into the great desire of God for people to worship Him.

"But the hour is coming, and is now here, when the true worshipers will worship the Father in spirit and truth, for the Father is seeking such people to worship him" (John 4:23, ESV).

Every believer has been called to worship.

In Jesus' dialog with the Samaritan woman, He used the verb *"worship," proskuneo*, seven times. Whenever we see something in Scripture repeated this much, we must realize that it is of major importance. The woman was worried about the differences in the worship locations of the Samaritans and the Jews. Jesus' answer to the woman indicated that the issue is not the place of worship but the object and the heart of worship. *"Jesus said to her, 'Woman, believe me, the hour is coming when neither on this mountain nor in Jerusalem will you worship the Father'"* (John 4:21, ESV). Proper worship is that which is focused on God and flows forth from the regenerated heart of the believer. This is the worship that glorifies God.

Worship is not restricted to specific times and places. Gibbs, in his treatise on worship, rightly designated in its title that worship is "the Christian's highest occupation" (Gibbs). Worship is the highest calling for every believer and it is one that is to occupy every moment and facet of the believer's life.

In the Bible there are many verbs translated as worship. In Jesus' discussion with the Samaritan woman, the word is *proskuneo*, which refers to prostrating oneself in homage (Strong G4352). It is the word used most often in the New Testament and is a picture of one bowing down before God as an expression of deep reverence. There are many other verbs translated as worship in the New Testament. Vine's Expository Dictionary presents the nuances of each of these. *Sebomai* means "to revere" stressing the feeling of awe or devotion. *Sebazomai* means to honor religiously. *Eusabeo* means "to act piously towards." A word that is used quite often is *latreuo*, which means "to serve, to render religious service or homage." (Vine) When we look at all these words combined, we see that worship covers the outpouring of the heart of a believer to God in every aspect of life. It includes reverence, homage, one's actions, and one's service.

In Romans we read these words regarding worship.

> *"I appeal to you therefore, brothers, by the mercies of God, to present your bodies as a living sacrifice, holy and acceptable to God, which is your spiritual worship"* (Romans 12:1, ESV).

Here the word for "*worship*" is the noun *latreia* that comes from the verb *latreuo*, which refers to rendering service (Strong G2999, 3000). It is in the context of believers presenting themselves as "*living sacrifices*" to God. The picture is one of the priests in the temple sacrificing animals to God for the people. They would slay the animals, which were offered to God on the altar. Here the believer is not to be slaughtered but to be a living sacrifice, presented holy and acceptable to God. This refers to a life given over to God, separated from the wrongful deeds of the flesh, and set apart for the glory of God. Worship is more than an event for the believer. It is the principal way of life.

Today many believers have relegated their worship to a weekly church event. Unfortunately, when they leave the event, they have no further consideration of God and His infinite greatness throughout the week. Moreover, many of those that relegate worship to a one-hour Sunday experience do not even enter true worship during that time. The reason is that they are mentally preoccupied with worldly things. Their purpose for participating on Sunday is not for the glory and honor of God because they are not vertically focused. The major reason for this is that their heart of worship was missing throughout the week. True worship that glorifies the Father is to be seen in the life of the believer every day irrespective of the place and the time.

The Reason Good Works Glorify God.

Previously, we understood that doing things to be seen by others was a problem. Yet Jesus tells us to do good works to be seen by others.

> *"Nor do people light a lamp and put it under a basket, but on a stand, and it gives light to all in the house. In the same way, let your light shine before others, so that they may see your good works and give glory to your Father who is in heaven."* (Matthew 5:15–16, ESV)

This might seem like a contradiction but it is not. This points directly to the issue of motives of which the dividing point is, "Who is receiving the glory?" Works that believers do with the motive of receiving earthly honor and glory for themselves will always miss the mark. This is the absolute wrong motive for good works. In fact, a work done with the express intent of self-glorification is not to be considered a good work. Only those works that are done for the glory of God are good. What makes good works glorifying to God? There are several scriptural principles for this.

Good works glorify God because it is Jesus' light shining through the believer. – When using a kerosene lamp the globe will often get sooty. While the light inside may be shining brightly the soot on the inside of the globe will prevent the light from shining out. Jesus told people to let the light shine out from them. By implication, Jesus' words tell us that all believers have a light to shine but they must do something to let it shine forth.

For believers to let this light shine out two things must be understood. They must clearly understand what this light is and then what will prevent it from shining out. Jesus' teaching presented vital truths regarding the source of this light. He stated, *"I am the light of the world. Whoever follows me will not walk in darkness, but will have the light of life"* (John 8:12, ESV). In His own words, He let us know that He was the true light of the world, a light shining in the darkness. John the Baptist said of Jesus, *"In him was life, and the life was the light of men. The light shines in the darkness, and the darkness has not overcome it"* (John 1:4–5, ESV). The only light that will penetrate the darkness of a sin fallen world is the light that radiates from the Son, Jesus Christ.

Moreover, Jesus stated something very pertinent to us, *"As long as I am in the world, I am the light of the world"* (John 9:5, ESV). Jesus was only in the world in a physical body for a very short time. After His resurrection it was the Father's plan for Jesus to return to heaven. He ascended to heaven some forty days after the resurrection. He left this world. Yet the light that would penetrate the darkness would not leave for good. This divine light would now come into the hearts of those who would truly believe. On the day of the Feast of Pentecost something happened in Jerusalem that changed the dynamic of the world. The light of Jesus came to dwell in every true believer by the ministry of the Spirit of God. Paul in his letter to the Romans affirmed the truth that the Spirit of Jesus indwells every true believer upon experiencing saving faith (Rom 8:9-11).

The Seven Filters

This is the light that Jesus wants every believer to shine into the world. It is not the believer's light but the light of Jesus in the believer. Paul wrote about this truth to the Galatians.

"I have been crucified with Christ. It is no longer I who live, but Christ who lives in me. And the life I now live in the flesh I live by faith in the Son of God, who loved me and gave himself for me." (Galatians 2:20, ESV)

He further wrote to the Corinthians regarding this same truth.

"But by the grace of God I am what I am, and his grace toward me was not in vain. On the contrary, I worked harder than any of them, though it was not I, but the grace of God that is with me." (1 Corinthians 15:10, ESV)

It was not Paul who was responsible for accomplishing all the great things that we attribute to him. It was the manifestation of God's grace, Christ in him, that accomplished so much. God is glorified in the believer's good works because He is doing them through the believer by the power of His Spirit. His light is shining through the believer to penetrate the darkness and glorify God.

This brings us to our responsibility. We are to let our light shine before men through good works. However, sometimes we tend to hide this light under a basket. The church that I pastored in Savannah had an additional Sunday ministry in a home for children ages 7 to 17. One time I had a mission team scheduled to minister there for a week during the Summer. In one of the assemblies, they had the children sing, "This Little Light of Mine." One of the things they would have the kids do is hold up their index finger to simulate a lit candle. I was standing in the back of the assembly and noticed one of the teens. He wanted to participate by holding up his index finger but did not want the other teens to see what he was doing. So, he held up his index finger of his right hand and hid it under his left armpit. I got a little chuckle out of this when they got to the lyrics, "Hide it under a bushel (no!)" Yet this young man demonstrated a problem we often see in Christendom today. Many will sing the song but not act it out.

What do believers need to do? In the earlier metaphor of the kerosene lamp, they needed to clean out the globe. What makes the globe of our lives dirty? There are many things. Pride is a big issue. We do not want to look weird to others. This is a problem of the flesh but not the only one. Sometimes our own wants, desires, and priorities can cause our lamp's globe to be covered with soot. Unrepentant sin is a huge issue. Believers need to examine themselves, confess sin, and repent to clean up their globes so the light will brightly shine through good works.

Good works glorify God because God has recreated believers to do them. – One of the skills the Lord gave me was to take things that were unusable and restore them to usefulness. It is a passion that I still have. Years ago, I wanted to restore an old car and I purchased an old dilapidated 1977 MGB convertible. It was bad. The tires were dry rotted, the top was caved in, the trunk was crinkled, it was filled with dirt and pine needles, and the neighborhood kids were using it for a jungle gym. My wife looked at it and must have thought I was crazy for buying it. I had it towed home and then got to take a deeper look at it. The exterior was the least of my problems. The brakes did not work, the fuel pump did not work, the clutch slipped, the exhaust system was shot, the suspension needed work, and the engine needed a rebuild. So, I went to work on the car and began fixing everything starting from the major internal components and systems.

The first thing I fixed was the fuel system and got the engine running. Then I worked on the clutch and brakes. It ran but because the exhaust fogged up the neighborhood, I rebuilt the engine. I also repaired the suspension items. I even upgraded the engine performance with new carburation, ignition components, performance camshaft, and exhaust. The car ran like a champ. Last, I took care of the outside and inside aesthetics, repairing rust spots, replacing the top, and repainting it. I drove that car for five years before I sold it for a profit since I needed money to buy groceries. The car was sort of my masterpiece. People looked at it and saw it as a showpiece. Similarly, every believer is a masterpiece of God's handiwork.

In his letter to the Ephesians Paul wrote the following.

"For we are his workmanship, created in Christ Jesus for good works, which God prepared beforehand, that we should walk in them" (Ephesians 2:10, ESV).

Our English word poem comes from the word translated *"workmanship," poiema*. It refers to something that is made (Vine). Every believer has experienced a special touch of the Master's hand for service. Before our salvation we were kind of like that junk MGB that I purchased. It could not function for its intended purpose. It was designed to transport people in a certain style but it could not. God created man in His image (Gen 1:27). That purpose was to be His representational on earth to bring glory and honor to Him. However, the fall of man in sin changed everything. It corrupted man in such a way that he could not perform the function for which God created him. When God saves people, He begins a rebuilding work within them so they will be able to function as designed. Paul wrote of this work in the life of believers.

"Do not lie to one another, seeing that you have put off the old self with its practices and have put on the new self, which is being renewed in knowledge after the image of its creator." (Colossians 3:9–10, ESV)

As believers we have a new identity in Christ. We have been transformed by His grace, new creations in Christ (2 Cor 5:17) and we are continuously *"being renewed in knowledge after the image of"* our *"creator."* God is doing the work in us to make us into beautiful vessels of honor for His glory. The only reason we are capable to fulfill this function of doing good works that glorify God is that He has rebuilt us into these vessels of honor. Believers are a visual display of God's glory.

They are good works because God has orchestrated them.

– My oldest grandson at the age of five wanted to learn how to fish. He went fishing with his dad once but did not catch anything. He thought that I was a master fisherman and would somehow get him to catch a fish. Frankly, I really did not know where the fish were or how to catch them in my area. I prayed hard and a few weeks before they visited, I spent time exploring the Moon River in my boat. I found a few spots that were fair but there was no guarantee. Then I saw something. There was one spot on the river where the birds were diving into the water. I slowly drove to that spot and began catching seatrout one after another. I went back every week and discovered a pattern in the fish run. When my grandson came to visit, I set up his rig and took him in the boat to that exact spot. Sure enough, he caught his first fish. He was super excited and I was filled with joy. While there really is no guarantee in fishing, there is an aspect of knowing what you are doing that greatly increases the odds. In a sense, by God's grace I was instrumental in getting my grandson on the fish.

It is normal for parents and grandparents to do everything within their power to make their children and grandchildren successful in what they do. In the same way, our heavenly Father seeks to make us successful in good works. In the Ephesians passage Paul wrote, *"we are his workmanship, created in Christ Jesus for good works, which God prepared beforehand."* Now no one can truly explain how God prepares these works beforehand for believers to do. God is sovereign over everything and this includes the good works that we are to do in our Christian lives. God has ordained the times when we reflect His glory for others to see. He has ordained our acts of mercy, forbearance, forgiveness, and many other acts of genuine love. He has ordained our service in the church when we greet people, work in the nursery, teach a class, help people to their seats, or tend to guests in the parking lot.

There is not one good work that a believer can do that is initiated by the will of the believer. No, every good work that a believer does has been orchestrated by the Sovereign Creator. The believer's part is to join God where He is already at work. That is why Paul stated that God created good works for us beforehand

The Seven Filters

"*that we should walk in them.*" God is glorified because He has done everything and given us the privilege to join Him in good works that He has prepared for us to do.

So, when we look at the motivation to do all things for the glory of God, we must give thanks. For God has done everything possible for us to succeed. He has placed the light of Christ in us, empowering us to do good works. He has recreated us in His image to be able to do good works. Moreover, He has created the good works for us to do.

If we consider all the blessings that God has showered upon us so that we might succeed in our Christian walk, how could we not have the motivation to glorify Him alone? Having the right motive of glorifying Him is the point of filter #6. The big question is this. "Is my motive to glorify God alone?" If you have any other motive you will fail to discern the thoughts and ideas you have in order to ensure they align with the will of God. *"So, whether you eat or drink, or whatever you do, do all to the glory of God."* (1 Corinthians 10:31, ESV)

Filter #1 – Am I living like a spiritual person?

Filter # 2 – Does God's word say it is ok?

Filter #3 – Are my methods correct?

(Am I seeking and doing the right things the right way?)

Filter #4 – Am I trusting the Lord or myself?

Filter #5 - What do other spiritual people think?

Filter #6 – Is my motive to glorify God alone?

Filter #7 – Am I absolutely certain?

"But whoever has doubts is condemned if he eats, because the eating is not from faith. For whatever does not proceed from faith is sin."
(Romans 14:23, ESV)

This is an old riddle that is solved by using logic. Imagine you are walking through the woods on a path to a destination. You must get to the destination but there is a fork in the road. You see a sign on the road just before the fork that says, "Danger One Road Leads to Certain Destruction." However, the sign does not tell you which road is the one leading to destruction and which road leads safely to your destination. Then you see two men near the intersection. You have been warned about the two men and know that one will always lie and never tell the truth. You also know that one will always tell the truth and never lie. They both know the path that leads to safety and the one that leads to destruction. The problem is that you do not know which one will tell you the truth and which one will tell you a lie. So how will you find out from the two men which road will lead you safely to your destination?

Well, I do not want you waiting here and failing to finish the book so I will give you the answer. You ask either one of the men this question. "Which way would the other man tell me is the safe way to go?" If you ask the man who could never lie, he would tell you exactly what the man who could not tell the truth would say. He would say, "He (referring to the man who would never tell the truth) would tell you the safe road is that one (the path to destruction)." If you asked the man who could not tell the truth and would always tell you a lie, he would give you the answer opposite to the one who would always tell the truth. He would say, "He (referring to the man that would never lie) would tell you the

The Seven Filters

safe road is that one (the path to destruction)." So, no matter who answered the question, "Which way would the other man tell me is the safe way to go?" you would always be pointed to the path of destruction. Thus, you would take the other path.

Well, if that rattled your brain go back to it later and sort through the logic. For now, let us just consider the big truth. Until you knew which road was the safe way you would not take either. This is the way we should use the final filter, "Am I absolutely certain?" If you are not certain, when discerning your thoughts and ideas to see what direction you should choose, you should wait until you are certain.

Decisions are Essential but Be Certain

It is a fact of life. Decisions are unavoidable. We must make them. Some are more critical than others. Earlier in this book we looked at Elijah's contest with the prophets of Baal on Mount Carmel. There we saw that the Jews of the Northern Kingdom were trying to worship both the one true God of Israel and the false god, Baal. Elijah took them to a point of decision. One that they had to make.

> "*And Elijah came near to all the people and said, 'How long will you go limping between two different opinions? If the* LORD *is God, follow him; but if Baal, then follow him.' And the people did not answer him a word.*" (1 Kings 18:21, ESV)

It is interesting that when Elijah asked them how long would they "*go limping between two different opinions?*" that they "*did not answer him a word.*" They could not make the decision that to us seems obvious. So, they stood at the place where there were two roads. One would lead to certain destruction and the other to blessing. Yet the answer to their dilemma would have been obvious if they knew the Scriptures and had true faith. Their problem was one of faithlessness.

Because they stood at the point of decision and would not or could not choose a path Elijah proposed a contest. It would be one between the prophets of Baal and himself to prove that the God of Israel was the true God. As you remember, in the contest Elijah and the prophets of Baal each built an altar and placed wood and a slain bull on it. Then each called upon their god to bring fire down on the altar. The prophets of Baal tried all day and failed. Then Elijah called upon the true God and fire came down from heaven and consumed the bull, the wood, all the water that Elijah used to saturate everything, and the stones of the alter so that nothing was left, not even the dust. At this display, the Israelites made their decision, *"they fell on their faces and said, 'The LORD, he is God; the LORD, he is God'"* (1 Kings 18:39, ESV).

Some decisions in life are relatively inconsequential. Choices like which shoe do I put on first or what shirt do I wear today have little consequence. Yet many of our choices are very significant. There is no choice more vital than that which is of eternal significance, which is to trust in Jesus Christ alone for eternal salvation. There are many others that are also vital in our lives. These are decisions such as how to serve the Lord, where to worship, choices of occupations, financial choices, relational choices, etc. When we have thoughts and ideas in these areas, we need to know that the decision we make is the right one. Therefore, we pass our thoughts and ideas through six filters.

Filter #1 – Am I living like a spiritual person?

Filter # 2 – Does God's word say it is ok?

Filter #3 – Are my methods correct?

    (Am I seeking the right things the right way?)

    (Am I doing the right things the right way?)

Filter #4 – Am I trusting the Lord or myself?

Filter #5 – What do other spiritual people think?

Filter #6 – Is my motive to glorify God alone?

After passing our thoughts through the six filters we come to the seventh, "Am I absolutely certain?" This is another filter of faith. It is the final question that we must ask ourselves. Until we know for certain we cannot and should not move forward.

God's Clear Direction

As we proceed with this filter, we must realize that God is not out to confuse us. In our decisions the direction He gives will always be clear. Paul in dealing with disorder in the Corinthian church's worship practices wrote this universal truth concerning the character of God. *"God is not a God of confusion but of peace. As in all the churches of the saints"* (1 Corinthians 14:33, ESV).

When I was in the Army Ranger School each of those in training were given an opportunity to lead several combat patrols. Some of the leaders were good and others were not. The ones that were the worst could not give clear and understandable instructions. I remember one patrol where the leader kept shouting out commands but they were unintelligible. We were in a total state of confusion and because of this he failed the mission. God does not operate like this. It is totally contrary to His nature to confuse His children.

Paul wrote to the church at Corinth regarding their abuses of worship (1 Cor 14). The problem was their disorderly use of the sign gifts in corporate worship. Parishioners were popping up and speaking out in a tongue or prophecy in a way that was disruptive to the worship experience. It was especially confusing to those who visited from the outside. To this issue Paul presented a vital truth regarding the character of our God. He is not the author of confusion. He will never direct us in a confusing manner. Believers must remember this principle when sorting out their thoughts and ideas in order to choose a course of action. If they are confused their confusion is not from God. This means that believers must have clarity. Thus, the question every believer must eventually ask is, "Am I absolutely certain?"

When Paul was on his second missionary journey, he ran into a decision point. He had planned to go into the province of Asia to preach the word. Yet the Holy Spirit forbid him to speak the word there. Then he and the team "*attempted to go into Bithynia, but the Spirit of Jesus did not allow them*" (Acts 16:7, ESV). At that stage Paul did not know what to do. What did he do? He did not proceed to do anything immediately. Instead, he went to Troas and waited for direction. There in the night he had a vision of a man in the province of Macedonia urging him to come and help the people there. From the vision Paul and his team confidently determined their next step.

"*And when Paul had seen the vision, immediately we sought to go on into Macedonia, concluding that God had called us to preach the gospel to them*" (Acts 16:10, ESV).

Paul and his missionary team made a firm decision that they were to go to Macedonia and left immediately. There was no confusion and they went without any doubt.

The point is this. When God directs us, it is clear. Until you are certain regarding the thoughts and ideas you have do not act upon them. In due season God will make things clear as you pray and seek His will in the Scriptures.

Faith and Decisions

When we travel in life, we will see many warning signs. On the road we will often see warning signs that might say sharp curve ahead, watch out for falling rocks, etc. We pay attention to these because they warn us of pending dangers. In making important decisions we also have a big warning sign. It is doubt.

In Paul's letter to the Christians in Rome he wrote about the problem of having doubts in decision making. The believers struggled with differing opinions in questionable areas such as eating and drinking. Regarding these issues he wrote the following.

The Seven Filters

"*whoever has doubts is condemned if he eats, because the eating is not from faith. For whatever does not proceed from faith is sin*" (Romans 14:23, ESV).

The problem was that if they doubted in one of these areas, they were not making a choice based on faith. Decisions not based upon faith constitute sin. This principle also applies to the way we respond to the thoughts and ideas we have in life. Should I, or shouldn't I? This is one of the most plaguing questions that many, including myself, have dealt with over the years.

There are certain situations where we do have to make immediate decisions. When I was in the military as a platoon leader on field maneuvers, I would have to make immediate decisions. These were based upon the changing situations we encountered and there was no time to delay. I would lead the platoon to take immediate action based upon my best assessment of the situation at the time. We must often make quick decisions in life. Yet even in these situations there is always time to pray for the Lord's guidance and blessing as we make our decisions. Granted it would be much better if we had time for prayerful and diligent contemplation but this is not always the case. Yet in most of our important decisions we have time to consider our options. In other words, we can take the time necessary to process our thoughts and ideas.

When I pastored the church in Savannah there came a time when I had to make a major change. It was a situation in which there was time to consider all the options and to diligently seek the Lord through prayer and His word. Changes in our convention's policies forced our church to move from our meeting place. This completely altered our vision for the ministry. We attempted to recast the vision for the church but were unable to adequately do so. This resulted in the closing of the church that I had planted. This was a difficult time for me and I needed to seek the Lord for direction.

After closing the church, I needed to know what vocational direction I should pursue. I had several thoughts. One was to go back to full time engineering in the paper converting industry. The other was to pursue what I believed to be God's calling on my life for pastoral ministry. I sent two resumes to companies looking for people with my engineering skill set. I immediately received a call from one company that offered me a great opportunity. I also sent resumes to many churches. I heard nothing from any of these churches. I truly struggled in the decision-making process. I thought, "Should I pursue the engineering job or continue to seek the pastorate?" Because I was not certain I did nothing and continued to pray and seek guidance from the Lord.

After much prayer I realized that I just could not give up the calling that God had for me. I turned down the engineering opportunity and continued to search for the right place for ministry. Soon afterward I received a call from a church in New Hampshire. I was certain that this was where the Lord wanted me. After a process of interviews and visiting the church, they called me as their pastor. We moved there and experienced one of the most blessed times of ministry as I had the privilege of watching the Lord build up that congregation.

Ultimately, having certainty in discerning our thoughts and ideas is an issue of faith. Let us not forget, as mentioned in Filter #4, that true faith is not trusting in oneself and it is not presumption. True faith is trusting in the Lord to give clear direction according to His will. Thus, believers must be assured to the best of their ability that their decisions align with God's will. Paul alluded to this principle in writing to the believers in Rome (Rom 14:13-23). Here the issue was one of eating and drinking (v17). Some believers would eat meat and others would not. Apparently, some would drink wine and others only water. There were significant differences of opinions on these things. Paul wrote to them that they should exercise caution in what they eat and drink because of the person who does not have faith to partake in those things. He did not want the liberty of some to cause another to stumble (v20-21).

The Seven Filters

Paul went on to give us many principles in this area. The first was that those who had faith to participate in an area where another believer had a different opinion should keep their faith between themselves and God. They were to be discrete. Then he presented this universal principle, *"whoever has doubts is condemned if he eats, because the eating is not from faith. For whatever does not proceed from faith is sin"* (Romans 14:23, ESV). In short, if we are not certain regarding our thoughts and ideas, we should not proceed to act upon them until we are.

When I pastored, I had plenty of people come to me for advice. Most often regarding issues of opinion. Many wondered if it was alright for them to drink wine or beer on occasion. While it is clearly wrong to partake in excess and become inebriated, the question regarded whether it was permissible to partake in moderation. I know some may not like the way I handled this but I would ask them, "Why do you ask?" They would tell me because they were uncertain. Then I would say, "If you are uncertain do not do it." Why? Because it is a matter of faith. If they are uncertain as to whether it is permissible or not, they would be sinning against their own conscience to partake. If you are not certain as to whether your thoughts and ideas are within the will of God do not act upon them until you are.

Waiting Patiently

I really like waiting. Not! I do not like waiting. One of the things that used to really get my goat was going to a fast-food restaurant and not getting food fast. We go to the fast-food restaurant not for the ambiance and not for gourmet food but for the fast service. We want average edible food for an average price served quickly. Thus, it sometimes gets frustrating when waiting for fifteen or twenty minutes in line to get fast-food.

I do not think any of us are good at waiting. I really should be better than this when you consider that some of my ancestors were from the United Kingdom. They are the masters of queuing, that is lining up and waiting. They seem so peaceful just standing in a line and doing nothing but waiting. I guess it is a way of life. I also guess that they are internally just as frustrated with waiting as I am. However, their outward demonstration of patience is admirable and an example for us.

Waiting is one of the believer's greatest expressions of faith. It takes great faith to wait on God. Isaiah wrote this wonderful verse of strength and encouragement for us who often must wait.

> *"Even youths shall faint and be weary, and young men shall fall exhausted; but they who wait for the Lord shall renew their strength; they shall mount up with wings like eagles; they shall run and not be weary; they shall walk and not faint."* (Isaiah 40:30–31, ESV)

All people get tired of waiting. Yet waiting on the Lord is different. Those who wait on the Lord gain strength in their waiting. God uses waiting to grow us in our faith, our ability to trust Him.

In many cases we will find ourselves without clear direction. We have an issue. We have a lot of thoughts and ideas regarding what to do about it. Yet we are uncertain as to the proper course of action. In this situation we must wait. What are we to do while we are waiting? Let us look at a very familiar example of waiting from the Scriptures.

Just prior to Jesus ascending to heaven He told His disciples to wait in Jerusalem for the promise of the Holy Spirit (Acts 1:4-5). So, they waited in an upper room in Jerusalem. Luke recorded what they did.

> *"All these with one accord were devoting themselves to prayer, together with the women and Mary the mother of Jesus, and his brothers"* (Acts 1:14, ESV).

There were in number about 120 believers that gathered and were devoted to prayer. They were seeking the will of God. Then suddenly, on the day of the Feast of Pentecost, the Holy Spirit came upon them and they were all filled with the Spirit. This work

The Seven Filters

of the Spirit initiated many remarkable things in Jerusalem. On that day Peter preached the first sermon and about three thousand who were gathered for the feast believed and were baptized.

The lesson for us is this. While we are waiting for direction we should be continually in prayer, seeking God in His word for the guidance we need. James wrote, *"If any of you lacks wisdom, let him ask God, who gives generously to all without reproach, and it will be given him"* (James 1:5, ESV). James wrote this in the context of going through various trials (James 1:2-8). There are many tremendous trials that we encounter in life. One of our greatest trials comes in those times of waiting on the Lord when we need direction. There is a purpose in our waiting and in these times, we should pray for wisdom and strength.

In Portsmouth, we had a prayer meeting with some of the local pastors once per month. We grew to be a tight bunch. At one of our Thursday prayer meetings one of the pastors let us know that he had just lost his position as an associate pastor in one of the area's largest churches. He asked for prayer in seeking the Lord's will regarding what he should do next. He had many ideas but did not know for certain what the best choice might be. We prayed for him and he continued to seek the Lord. Month after month we continued to meet and I would ask him again, "Has the Lord revealed anything to you yet." He would reply, "No, I haven't heard a thing from the Lord." Later he sensed the Lord's leading to pursue an advanced degree in ministry, which he did. Yet he still needed direction for what he was to do in ministry. So, he kept on praying and seeking the Lord. Finally, a year or so later, the Lord led him to begin an itinerant ministry that the Lord used to greatly bless many congregations. He had to wait on the Lord but was rewarded with clear direction.

The point of the story is this. When we are not certain regarding the actions that we should take in response to our thoughts and ideas, we must continue to seek wisdom from the Lord through prayer and the word of God. We should continue to run our thoughts through the filters until we can pass through the seventh and final one, "Am I absolutely certain?"

Having Peace About a Decision

There is one other big point that we must discuss before wrapping up the seventh filter. It is a potential trap having to do with the concept of having peace about a decision. Often when people have decided to do something they will say, "I have peace about it." This methodology of determining whether our actions are in the will of God or not is very often misused. When many people state, "I have peace about it," it means that they feel at ease with their decision. What is the down side of this? They can let their own desires affirm their decision. The man that I mentioned earlier in this book who left his wife and moved in with the girl next door had peace about it. Yet there is no way that what he did aligned with the will of God for him. So, we need to understand peace in the context of making godly decisions regarding our thoughts and ideas.

Paul wrote to the church in Colossae, "*And let the peace of Christ rule in your hearts, to which indeed you were called in one body. And be thankful*" (Colossians 3:15, ESV). The verb in this verse translated "*rule,*" *brabeuo*, means to arbitrate and comes from a word that refers to an umpire (Strong G1018). Paul correctly indicated that the "*peace of Christ*" should be an umpire in our lives. It should be the umpire of our hearts. Paul further presented this thought in his writing to the Philippians regarding how to deal with anxiety.

> "*do not be anxious about anything, but in everything by prayer and supplication with thanksgiving let your requests be made known to God. And the peace of God, which surpasses all understanding, will guard your hearts and your minds in Christ Jesus.*" (Philippians 4:6–7, ESV)

Here too the "*peace of God*" is to guard the believer's heart and mind. The misapplication of this idea of having peace about a decision is a subtle trap into which people may easily fall. There is a distinct difference between the "*peace of God,*" and the "*peace of*

The Seven Filters

man." The phrase, "*the peace of man*" can be rephrased to mean "*the peace of the flesh*" or "*the peace of the world*," neither of which equals "*the peace of God.*" The "*peace of God*" is that peace that satisfies the desires of the Spirit. The "*peace of God*" will never ever be misaligned with the moral precepts of God's word. The "*peace of God*" will always align with the righteousness of God and will never be contrary to it.

So, after negotiating the first six filters, we must make a final decision. It must be one in which we have full confidence. In other words, we must be certain that it is the direction that aligns with the will of God for us. Thus, we pass our thoughts and ideas through the seventh filter, "Am I absolutely certain?" After doing so we will have filtered out the things that do not align with the will of God. What remains should be one clear and decisive response. It is upon this that we shall move forward with due diligence.

What happens if we are still not certain, if we are still divided in our ideas? In this case, we continue to pass these remaining thoughts through the seven filters until we have the confidence we need.

The Seven Filters

Filter #1 – Am I living like a spiritual person?

Filter # 2 – Does God's word say it is ok?

Filter #3 – Are my methods correct?

(Am I seeking and doing the right things the right way?)

Filter #4 – Am I trusting the Lord or myself?

Filter #5 – What do other spiritual people think?

Filter #6 – Is my motive to glorify God alone?

Filter #7 – Am I absolutely certain?

(Do I have the peace of God about this?)

Conclusion

We have considered seven filters for discerning our thoughts and ideas to ensure they align with the will of God. Sorting through the seven filters may take time and effort as you seek to know God's will. This is not easy but it is essential. The effort will pay dividends in experiencing *"the peace of God."* Even though there is no guarantee for a life without struggles, by passing your thoughts and ideas through the filters you will generally make better decisions in life and make fewer mistakes.

When you get through the six filters and come to the seventh you must ask yourself, "Am I absolutely certain?" If you are not certain, pass your ideas through the filters once again and again until you are certain. Yes, in some cases you may not have a lot of time to wait. For you need to make some decisions immediately. Yet this is the rarity and even in these situations there is always time to pray as you choose a course of action. However, in most major decisions you will have time to prayerfully contemplate your thoughts and ideas. You will have time to pass them through the seven filters.

While you are waiting to hear from the Lord regarding direction in your thoughts and ideas, never forget that you are always present where the Lord wants you. He wants to use you right where you are. Do not make the error of falling asleep in the faith until you have clear direction. God calls all believers to live by faith, in every moment, wherever they may find themselves (2 Cor 5:6-7). Serve the Lord where you are and wait on Him for direction regarding the thoughts and ideas you have for the big decision.

The Seven Filters

One time a man told me that as soon as his financial situation got better, he would serve the Lord. The only problem with this was that his situation would likely never get better. Others have stated they were looking for a place of service and planned to move to another area as soon as they figured it out. My counsel was always the same. I would tell them, "Until you know for certain that you should change your direction in life, serve the Lord where you are right now." Stay on the correct biblical course you have been following and make no changes until the options are clear and you are certain.

One last thought. As you practice using the seven filters, in time they will become natural to you. In other words, you will not labor as much in your decision making. Consider this obvious example from my life.

One day I was driving home from the factory that I managed. It was late. It was summer time in Savannah Georgia. I was tired. As I drove down the road to my home, I would pass a nursing home on the right-hand side of the road. One day I saw a man at the end of the driveway with one leg amputated sitting in a wheelchair. Honestly, the Lord spoke to me that I should stop and talk to that man and share the good news with him. However, I was tired and drove right on by without stopping. I got home and felt the full weight of guilt for not stopping. I spent a very uncomfortable evening praying, confessing, and repenting for my failure. I knew. I just knew that the Lord wanted me to speak with that man. I told the Lord that if I ever saw that man again, I would stop and speak with him. I learned my lesson.

The point is that sometimes we will fail in our decision making. Yet, God is faithful. Confess your failures and determine to do better the next time. Do not give up using the seven filters for repetitive usage will result in better actions.

I drove down that road home from work past the nursing home every weekday for months. A year went by and I never saw that man. Then one evening as I was driving home from work, there he was. I was driving so fast that I went right by the nursing home. The Lord put it on my heart to turn around. At the next safe opportunity, I did so. I caught up with the man as he was about 50 feet from going back into the building. I stopped by him and said hello. Then I handed him a pocket testament with the statement, "I want to give you the most . . ." He took the words out of my mouth and finished my sentence, "the most important book anyone can read." I said, "Yes, it is." Then I asked, "But, have you reached a place in your spiritual life where you know for certain that if you died you would go to heaven?" He answered, "No, but I always wanted to know the answer to that question." I then shared the message of the gospel with him and he received Christ.

A week later I went back to the home to follow up with the man. I drove in and parked the car and walked up the ramp to the door. He met me at the door and said, "Come in here." He led me into one of the rooms with several beds. Entering the room he said, "Tell these guys exactly what you told me." He had these men in the room waiting for me to arrive. I shared the message with them and they all received Jesus also. A week later one of the men in the room went on to be with Jesus.

Yet the story has even a deeper part. I shared this testimony at our church a few weeks later during a sermon. After the service a younger woman in the congregation came up to me in tears. She asked me, "Was that a man with one leg amputated sitting in a wheelchair in the driveway of the nursing home on White Bluff Road?" I said, "Yes it was." She said, "A little over a year ago, I saw that man in that wheelchair. The Lord told me to begin praying for him to be saved. You are the answer to those prayers."

You see the Lord does speak to us. He does so through the "*still small voice*" of our thoughts and ideas. However, it is possible to be deceived. In the case of this story of the man in the wheelchair, the answer was obvious. Yes, it is absolutely in agreement with the will of God for us to pray specifically for a man to be saved and to spread the good news of salvation. Yet knowing the good thing to do is only half the battle. When we have discerned that it is the Lord speaking to us, we must act in accordance with His will in doing the good work to which He has called us.

My closing exhortation to you is to use the seven filters. Practice them and make them a part of your life. The more you use them, the more natural and better your decision-making processes will become. Continue to use the seven filters to discern your thoughts and ideas to ensure they agree with the will of God. By doing so you will experience the joy of bringing glory to God through your good works.

Works Cited

Barna Group. "The State of the Bible: 6 Trends for 2014." 8 April 2014. *Barna Group Website*. Document. 26 October 2022.

Carson, D.A. "The Ground of Our Assurance - Don Carson." 27 January 2016. *https://www.youtube.com/watch?v=sJRz5fLCmM8*. 3 November 2022.

Chafer, L.S. *He That is Spiritual*. Wheaton: Van Kampen Press, 1918.

—. *Systematic Theology*. Dallas: Dallas Theological Seminary, 1947-48.

Craig, Anne. *Discovery of 'thought worms' opens window to the mind*. 13 June 2020. Article - Queen's Gazette. 24 October 2022.

Gibbs, Alfred P. *Worship: The Christian's Highest Occupation*. Kansas City: Walterick Publishers, n.d. Paperback.

Goodreads. *Goodreads*. 2022. 1 11 2022.

Lake, rebecca. "Television Statistics: 23 Mind-Numbing Facts to Watch." 14 July 2022. *CreditDonkey*. Article. 4 February 2023.

Muller, George. *Georgemuller.org*. 9 May 2016. Computer. 12 October 2022.

Pierson, Arthur Tappan. *George Mueller of Bristol*. London: James Nisbet & Co., 1899.

Removed at request. *Understanding Media and Culture*. Minneapolis: University of Minnesota Libraries Publishing Edition, 2016. Digital PDF.

Steinberg, Charles Side. *Mass Media and Communication*. Hastings house, 1972.

Strong, James. *A Concise Dictionary of the Words in the Hebrew Bible*. Nashville, New York: Abington Press, 1890. Electronic.

—. *Strong's Exhaustive Concordance*. Public Domain, 1890.

Taylor, Justin and D.A. Carson. "A Gospel Moment on YouTube: D.A. Carson on the Two Jews Talking the Day Before the First Passover." 12 October 2021. *The Gospel Coalition*. 3 November 2022.

Thayer. *Greek-English Lexicon to the New Testament*. Boston: H.L. Hastings, 1896.

Vine, W.E. *Vine's Complete Expository Dictionary of Old and New Testament Words*. 1940.

Westminster. *The Shorter Catechism*. Cornhill: Thomas and John Fleet, 1765.

About the Author

Steven Hankins is passionate about the health of local churches. The Lord saved Steve in 1983 while reading a Gideon Bible in a hotel room. He later answered the Lord's call to the pastorate. Steve has over 40 years of leadership experience in the military, industry, and the pastorate. He received a B.S. in Mechanical engineering from Drexel University and an M. Min., D. Min., and Th.D. from Covington Theological Seminary. He taught theology and Bible in Covington's Savannah extension for six years. Steve has held many ministerial positions including serving as a director of evangelism, single adult ministries, young couples ministries, interim-pastor, church-planter and pastor, and senior pastor. His last position was as the senior pastor at Seacoast Community Church in New Hampshire, where he served the Lord in church renewal and revitalization. Today, he currently maintains a daily devotional commentary on books of the Bible at www.renewingtheheart.org. His great passion is to help churches and pastors who have reached a point of discouragement find renewed hope by experiencing spiritual renewal and revitalization.

Made in the USA
Columbia, SC
03 November 2024